My Husband's Roses

My Husband's Roses

one−page poems

Susanna Lee

R o s e M a s o n P r e s s

Douglassville, PA USA

10 9 8 7 6 5 4 3 2 1

Rose Mason Press, an imprint of HPL Publications,
PO Box 564, Douglassville, PA 19518
USA

ISBN: 978-1-61305-032-3

Library of Congress Control Number: 2021952100

Library of Congress Cataloging-in-Publication Data

Lee, Susanna, 1956 –
My Husband's Roses / Susanna Lee
            p. cm.
ISBN:978-1-61305-032-3
I. Title
PS3621.H87L44
811'.6-dc23   2021952100

Summary: Close observation captures moments in poetry.

Subjects: Poetry; Poetry -- Authorship; Lee, Susanna --
Poetry; American poetry -- 21st century.

Tags: poetry, American poetry.

Cover photo by Susanna Lee.

Dedication

To my husband, who often tells our children he is happy
he can make so much money so their mom can play poetry.

Contents

One-Page Poems

One-Page Poems (cont.)

One-Page Poems (cont.)

One-Page Poems (cont.)

One-Page Poems (cont.)

one–page poems

A Bed of Roses

The Neighborhood Beautification Committee never finds anything to put on its agenda.

Everything is within reach.

Human skin never touches plastic.

Delicious foods are all nutritious.

The autoharp sounds as angelic as crickets.

Every day, we celebrate the moment we came into this world.

Ghosts of the dead make pleasant conversation at our dinner table.

Silence is never strained.

Kissing switches on the ability to read minds.

No one ever throws up.

All sleep is sound sleep.

Time is expandable and retractable as origami.

The moon tucks us in at night.

Eating ice cream makes us physically fit.

Hindsight improves the appearance of nothing.

A Cheery Poem

I subscribe to seduction by butterfly kisses,
yet I'm denied skin-on-skin contact far too often.

Growing old, my bed cold, my cheery thoughts are of death.

I've read up on poets and suicide,
razors and rivers, acid and nooses,
and the latest in medical research.

I could try underexertion
and combine that with reckless medication noncompliance.
That ought to do the trick.
How long have I got, if I ignore my doctor's advice?

I could get a tattoo.
Dicey needle and unregulated ink.
Could take years, but it would take me out, don't you think?

I could die of malnutrition.
My fridge is already filled with "nothing to eat."
To hurry it along, I could nibble nothing but Twinkies.
I've done it before for an entire week.

What about bacteria?
I'll eat my salad before I check the news
to see if today's romaine from California
has salmonella.

Yet, the odds are slim that lettuce alone will do me in.

Eating bacon is lethal!

Or, maybe not. It depends on the latest research.

I'll wait until bacon-hating comes back in fashion,
then I'll simply eat bacon and wait.

A Girl Goes Missing

It's late winter.
Any day now, the robins will return.
They always do.
At least, some of them do.

I scan the sky and trees outside my picture window.
Not yet.

It's windy out.
It looks cold.

I'm back to scanning my small screen.
I'm keeping up with the world outside my living room.
Here's a message on social media,
"Missing from rehab, a teen girl."
The state police page pleads, *"Please share!"*
There's her picture there, and everything.

I don't know her.
Never saw her before in my life.

Or, maybe I did. Who can tell?
She's hiding under layers of makeup,
especially around the eyes.

I hit the "Share" button.
This perfect stranger,
hiding in dark eye shadow and black eyeliner,
won't know this stranger tries to save reckless kids
from their own innocent inclinations.

Years later, she'll tell her kids,
"Be smart! Don't . . ."

She'll leave unfinished, *". . . do what I did."*

She hopes they'll be lucky, too.

A Nightmare While Awake in the Dark

Fig.
Gift.
Pffft!

Her workshop poems leave me in tears
which erupt in the car on the way home from Rutherford
every Tuesday evening of every week
and every time haunt me the next morning
with their cats clawing and screeching in the hot August night
while bloody mice lay dismembered on the sidewalk.

I am five and frightened, with no grown-ups near,
but a monster enters my bedroom
in a silhouette that looks like my dad's.

But, it's silent. It's not him.

I can't count when I'm scared.
It's the dark of night.
Nothing is on the chifferobe ...

... but aliens from outer space are draining all life from Earth!

Moon shadows,
streaks of car lights,
gleaming satin ribbons
stream over my twin bed, across the wall and ceiling.

My sister lies lifeless on the other bed,
the one under the window,
the window devoid of curtains.

My parents are somewhere distant, far away,
unavailable,

strapped into the depths of hell . . .

A Plea/Bargain Proof

*Folks, I need some quotes about my work for the
back of my next chapbook Ektomorphic, a chapbook
of ekphrasis. I know I can count on y'all. Thanks.*

—Ron Bremner

The 13th incarnation of the Dalai Lama slit open the belly of the
whale with his Swiss army knife and released himself into the
Horse Latitudes, then swam to Norway. Exhausted, he hitched
a ride on a Stanley Steamer with a school of sardines headed for
Newark's Ironbound District. He begged a burner phone from
a sympathetic crack dealer so he could order up a Ron Bremner
poem for curbside pickup. He ate it. It tightened his abs. The
lack of a fully-functional player piano is never a problem within
a Ron Bremner poem. The thought of roughing up one of his
poems occurred to me, but I crawled under a rock, and in three
days the urge had vaporized. Ron Bremner wrote Miss Piggy
a love poem. To quote Shakespeare, "Ron Bremner's poems
make a mockery of all that reeks of surety." I swivel on my
barstool, eat crow, and bask in Ron Bremner's lines. As I bloat
up like a Baby Trump balloon floating over the Thames, the last
Ron Bremner line I read burps into the microphone and says,
"Excuse me! I noticed you haven't touched your pickle. Are you
going to eat that?" I see in the mirror over the milkshake
machine a Ron Bremner line tangled in the chain of his pocket
watch hanging from his zoot suit. **Goo!** I *long* for Catalina salad
dressing. As I get up to go, I leave on my plate an unopened
paper straw and a slightly sticky Ron Bremner line. The
waitress sees what I've done and writes me up for honesty. The
guys who work in the kitchen come out to take selfies with me.
I leave the waitress and staff this generous tip:

>"Buy Ron Bremner's book, ya bastids!"
>"Buy Ron Bremner's book, ya bastids!"
>"Buy Ron Bremner's book, ya bastids!"

A Toast: To Bashō's Eyes

To the ancient poet Bashō!

To Bashō's keen vision!

To his intense focus on the world he inhabited!

To his acute observations,
made with the very essence of his being!

To his recording of his observations!

To his deep insight!

To his creation, his poetry!

To his passion!

To his choice to indulge his passion!

To his conscious action!

To his sharing of his poetry!

To Bashō, inspiring leader,
who showed us how we may discover!

To a life of beauty and wonder!

To our seeing, through Bashō's eyes!

Addicted to Poetry

Hello, my name is Susanna, and I am addicted to poetry.
When I hear your words, fellow poets, my mind begins
to roil and a zing! stings my heart. My brain, willing
accomplice, shoots me with endorphins. This keeps me
returning, begging for more.

At home, I struggle. My mind's basest objectives begin
to ferment, and I sift phrases for rising intention. I hone
the points of phosphorus-drenched arrows designed
to incinerate your own shrieking demons. At open mic,
I ignite all in my quiver at once and let fly. I aim for
the hardened void of our shared, stunned silence.

I fill page after page with distilled shots of whine,
aged to perfection, mellowed with time.

I'm brachiating with arboreal primates, hanging with the forest
canopy, grasping line after line. I'm filling urns with the dust
of the moon gone awry. While I'm showering or driving or
paying bills online—hey, every day and almost all the time—
I'm stupefied, wrassling words to deal your next high.

I even score "bacon" for you: sizzling hot, crisp.
It's snapping, burning my eyes, my lips, my fingertips.

Should I fail to appear here, you'll know I've hit poetry bottom.
Dragged from a poetry den, I'm in treatment to cure this
obsession. I'm in a small room, painting still life from memory,
"Watermelon with Elephants."

I've a ridiculous fascination with words. It's gotten so bad, I'm
waterskiing with toads in pink boas off the beaches of Guam.

I need poetry detox.

After the Night Passes

After the breath recognizes
it's got another chance

After the time is verified
"waking hours"

After the Weather and Facebook and the BBC agree
no terrors lay in ambush

After yesterday's traumas
get back in the queue

After the medicine goes down with a sip of water
okay

After the feet touch the floor
okay

After the toilet bowl reports
peeing still works

Coffee
High-fiber cereal

Boot up
Log in

Read
Reflect

Coffee
Reply

I'm still here
for the moment

Is my book in print yet

After the Passings

"After the Passings," by Miss Emily Dickinson

I miss stroking

   —   soft hair

  —   gentle sliding

    —   my finger

      gliding down

     —   a   rosy   cheek

     my fingers   damp

—   tears, brushed away

  the   skipping

—   *gay* skipping —

       at   *play!* —

Amidst Desolate Cries, Choose Joy Abundant

If I am awakened before dawn, I love to go downstairs,
open the windows, and listen to the mourning dove.
Sit on the couch. Sip my coffee.
Drink in the sky over the forest beyond the pond.
Absorb the song's intermittent, poignant, low-keyed notes.
The cadence matches my mood in the darkness.

Through the picture window, I face the world,
trying to remember all that's transpired in my life,
everything from the beginning
right up to the moment I fell asleep the night before.

I recall my motivation for continuing my existence,
where I left off in the creation of my story.

I contemplate. Recall past mistakes.

Then, gratitude.
Then, courage to start anew.

Dawn breaks over the unfolding scene
revealed by the rising sun.

Day sweeps in, pours over my soul.

one mourning dove
brightening yellow sunbeams
dawn's unfolding joy

Bad Minor Poet Blues

I try writing poems.
I've got the Bad Minor Poet Blues.
Oh, yes, I try writing poems.
I've got the Bad Minor Poet Blues.
I've got a pen and a piece of paper.
Sweat from every pore, it sure does ooze.

I try my hand at free verse, but I've got the Bad Minor Poet
Blues. Oh, yes, this is one, you see? Doesn't rhyme or nothin'.
It's free. This poem gets worse and worse and worse.
I've got the Bad Minor Poet Blues.

Can't catch a rhyme in this poetry net of mine.
Troubles, I want to shriek about.
Wrongs of the world to right, to write about.
Don't know which, dear God, to make a poem of . . .

. . . and my eighth-grade English teacher would have
a bird if she knew I used a cliché, or a preposition
to end a sentence with, or wrote a poem without rhyme
or meter in it, with no poetic form or any synecdoche
or some other God-forsaken rule of poetry
I never did learn how to use . . .

So now, this poem's cooking,
but I don't know which poetic form I'll abuse.
I've got this delicious honey pot of a poem brewing.
Yet, I can't decide which words and which lines to choose.
If I knew my meter from my prose from my Shakespeare
from my bloomin' arse, this wouldn't be so hard to do.

If I knew what a synecdoche was,
I'd know exactly which form to choose.

I've got the Bad Minor Poet Blues,
mad bad Bad Minor Poet Blues.

Basking in Boxes of Old Stuff

My corner of Eden … lying out on the lawn
   on a beach towel in the hot July sun … afternoon, no breeze

… braising in Johnson's Baby Oil

… no school for two whole months

… a pile of my brother's comic books,
                            and he's at camp

… my transistor radio, tuned to Cousin Brucie
                 and his picks, "Cousin Bruce Morrow!"

> *Why do you build me up, build me up,*
> *Buttercup, baby,*
> *just to let me down, let me down,*
> *and mess me around …*

It all rushes back, wafts in on the paper wrapper
           of a stick of Fruit Stripe Gum, an old bookmark
                in one of these unfinished tomes.
In each box in my attic, I have an encounter with an aroma.
My reaction to a whiff, even a faint trace, brings on a pop quiz:

> *Don't I belong to that place?*
> *Where am I now? And why am I not still at home?*

How long will it be before sitting alone with my stuff,
        going through boxes, picking through all that I own
               to throw out what I won't miss,
doesn't send me reeling, wrestling years of my past?

Long gone, the dancing, the falls, the beaches, the stars,
   the tents, the slow-burning crackling of campfires . . .

The smoke, I remember.
The flame, we once tended—you and I.

Belly Dancers

They look, but they don't touch the belly dancers.

Our practiced moves drive these men wild.
We groove, sway our hips, sidle from side to side
round and around the room.

Smooth!

Exotic costumes, sultry tunes, perfumes.
We exude our own scents, too.
Our graceful fingers sweep translucent veils past our lips.

My eyes peek out at the intimate crowd.
They're wowed.

I move. Free.
These men don't suspect . . .
my passion meets—no, surpasses!—theirs, in heat.

My cymbals, "Ting . . ."

A little ". . . ching! . . . ching! . . ."

Sweet!

It's nice to feel protected.
To be so strong.
So full of guile.

When my belly shakes, it makes men swoon.
Behind my veil, I smile.

A little . . . shake! shake! . . . of my hips.
A tingle.
A little . . . ching! ching! . . . of my cymbal.

That's all it takes to bring a man down to the ground.

Better Grandma

Baby, pull this crepey skin. Find my elbow.

Forget your shoes.
Free lawn-crawling gathers fresh germs to nourish your heart.

Swaddle, with me, this newborn wolf.
His canines will not bite you. Not yet.

Eat! What I put in your mouth has never touched metal.

Find your own cello, your voice, your own tambourine,
and you will find your America.

You will not be able to resist music
once you have made your own.

We need stars, to float in the night to keep the moon company
when the sun is tired of playing.

We will search underground and find one daffodil bulb
and be rich.

We play only imagination games.

We name our scars.

What is faith?
Watch half a wriggling earthworm.
The other half will grow back.
He has no eyes, yet no hunger. He lives in his supper.

Does a grown robin carry anything, anything at all?
He was once contained inside a fine, blue shell.
Then, he broke it!

To breathe.

Between a Concrete Floor and a Hard Place

Has news got out
that migrant kids in caravans from places south
who make it here
sleep on the floor and cry a lot?

Has word got out
that kids down south who don't come north
by bus or car or train or by walking far,
but stay at home,
sleep on the floor and cry a lot?

All wish they'd have good food to eat,
a place to wash their hands and feet,
a place to work to earn their keep,
and refuge from the cold.

Their loved ones, bought and sold,
or beat and maimed
or killed for speaking out.

They wait in line for freedom
while the death clock keeps on ticking,
their options all run out.

There must be something we could do
to save them from their awful fate.

Something. Something we could do.

For some,
it is too late.

Bite Me

I hide my entire body, from toe to chin, from biting bugs.
In even the hottest weather, I wear heavy jeans and knitted
sweaters with long sleeves and high necks, my protection
from flies, gnats, and mosquitoes. I ignore the wistful longing
of insects: their buzzing in my ears is merely a slightly
annoying humming, reeking of their base desire. I'm wrapped
in armor. Though they want to bite me, they won't get in.

I imagine mosquitoes must mourn my awareness of their
selfish plot to inject under my skin their clot-busting saliva,
to ease the flow of my blood into their pipes. But, I will
never again lie awake nights for weeks, tormented by the itchies
of a single bite.

I try to bear variations in weather temperature graciously,
without complaining. In winter, I'm really never too warm.
In summer, I'm fine in air-conditioning. Outside, at the ballpark,
as I root for the home team, I may be roasting on the bleachers
in the beating sun, but I know that by the end of the seventh-
inning stretch, after the sun has finally set, the ambient air
will settle down to a reasonable 72 degrees. I will be
comfortable and nothing on me will itch.

I dress to protect myself, but I notice men glare at the thick
fabric covering my breasts and shoulders and legs and ankles.
Other women are wearing v-necks or sheer tops or short skirts
and sandals. I hear men, disappointed, muttering about me
under their breath. They curse women like me, for hiding
the glory of our curves.

Women who cover up are such cruel beasts!
Who would selfishly deny a man the harmless gratification
of staring in ecstasy at naked female flesh?
It should be seen as an act of freedom, to be able to share
the view of one's beautiful, womanly body!

Male enjoyment, from looking at me in lust . . . simply
a pleasurable, victimless pastime . . . .

Bristol, Connecticut

There is an ideal place to live. A friend of mine described the town next over from hers, Bristol, Connecticut, where her high school tennis matches always ended in defeat. There, in Bristol, her school's football team was always trounced. The games were a massacre.

"When I have kids, I'm going to raise them in Bristol," she told me. "That's where the winners live."

That's where I'm going to go. I've always wanted to be where the air is sweet, where the water's clean, where the humming of bumblebees lifts the fog and frog song sings the morning sky into being. Where beautiful birds choose to build nests for their offspring.

It never occurred to me to plant the roots of my family tree with an eye towards avoiding defeat.

"The world is your oyster," I'd been told. "It doesn't matter where you live or where you grow old. You take yourself with you, wherever you go."

Not so. In Bristol, Connecticut, the streets are paved with gold medals. Kids grow differently where winners live. They thrive.

It may be too late for me and mine, but when my grandkids ask their Susanna Nana for advice—on where to work, where to live, and where to raise a family—I'll say, "Try Bristol, Connecticut. I've heard it's very nice."

Cacophony

After the cleaning crew departs with their mops, there remain,
on the spots they missed, tiny remnants of human beings, bits
of blood, or sticky bandages hidden by the random design
of the pseudo stones painted into the vinyl tile of the nursing
home floor. Peering down the corridor, one can see, lined up
in parade formation, a sprinkle of waiting seats, some with
cushions, some with wheels. Fixtures have been designed
as identical black boxes and appear as birds circling us from
their perches near the ceiling. As one croons unintelligible
country western music, from the next glares a bulb insufficient
to extinguish its assigned space of darkness. Under each
spotlight, a visitor's chair attends to its duty with apathy. Each
patient's room reels out its own aria. The cacophony of TVs!
Music, schlock, rock bands, commercials for cars, for
deodorants. Interminable talk shows. Never is such tedium
borne willingly at home. The insistent whine of enthusiastic
advertisers blends with the semi-silent, unattended groans
of each room's uncomfortable inhabitant. His dry-erase board
lays out a litany of his vitals and specifies the topping for his
breakfast toast. The passageways teem with mixed blessings:
warm embraces and tentative diagnoses. Well-hidden by the
high wall of green plastic shrubbery adorning the building's
entryway, family reunions bump into tearful farewells, much as
would-be-confessers bump into the newly-absolved at the doors
of every Catholic church. Each denies the possibility of their
co-existence—each might easily trade places with the other.
Not all who travel here will navigate the arduous trail back
to the front door. Fewer still know onto which path they will
be driven next. The odds are, you and I aren't boarded here.
This measure of physical breakage happened to someone else.
The stone patience of the unfortunate permanent residents
who bear this cacophony alone echoes around the walls
of the building, bumps along the railings lining the halls,
and brushes elbows with the long downward spiral of tears,
the wet paths of those once surrendered to this fortress.

Canvas

Preparing my brain to paint a fair "poem," I check out
my palette. The colors swim, thinly disguised on the plate.

I gesso with "Anger" and brush smooth the surface.
Isn't there room left for anything more?

I scoop out "Compassion." Well, a small dab is all I need.
A pinch of "Hope," sprinkled. I conserve "Hope," for next time.
I ladle on "Scribbles." "Procrastination."
"A bark from my puppy." He's scared of the rain.

Now, I add "My first lover." The pain, not the kisses.
This "Tenderness" comes from *The Gift of the Magi.*
"Tradition!" from *Fiddler.* "My seventh-grade algebra teacher."

I almost forgot to add
"That puddle I splashed in when I was a sixth-grader."

Some high school humiliation, "Laughing too loudly
when all of the other girls mocked Fran's red leaking."
I combine that with their whispers,
"She lives with her grandpa?"
"Yes, and they all live in terror. He beats them when drunk!"

Oy . . .

Some "poem" I've made up from beating the bushes
of nightmares that haunt me as I stare, awake.

I glare at "Injustice."
Wait, what?

"Cold, faithless husbands."
Why?!

"Mothers forgetting to tuck us in."
Goodnight!!!

Cascade

When Alzheimer's finally kicks in,
I will start to make sense.

When you see I'm no longer that poet on fire,
set me out on that ice floe.

I am still teetering on that fence
between creative expression and life's end,

trying my best to keep my words from nesting
like shimmery blue pigeons in a Brooklyn junkyard.

I feel like my grandmother, when she said,
"I'm sliding between death and a banana peel."

Draw a picture of me.
I'm a river, not a tree.

Not sure how to take me?
It's better to let me ride out on the E-Train by myself.

It was fun trying to write a poem
in the middle of the night.

Here's where it hurts
—I won't even know how this ends.

Caught by Poetry

My
experiences   try
to   escape   me.
I seek to   capture   the essence
of   each   one.
I   draw   them   back   to   me,
pull   them   close,
to   be   caressed,
again   and   again,
until   *I*   say
I   am   ready
to   let
go
.
(
)
/
(
)
(
\
)
/
(
)
_ .
(
\
)
(
)
.

Charles Bukowski Writes Poetry With Me

Charles Bukowski sings to me.
He can't hold a tune.
He's always off key.
His music is creepy,
but I'm never sleepy
when Charles Bukowski sings to me.

Charles Bukowski haunts this place,
my writing nook,
my sacred space.
Neck and neck
we're in this race.
Charles Bukowski haunts this place.

Charles Bukowski robs me blind.
He won't give it back
when I lend him a line.
He calls it "Mine!"
but I don't mind
when Charles Bukowski robs me blind.

Charles Bukowski steals my nerve.
When I think I can write,
he'll throw me a curve.
I might like a word
he'll kick to the curb.
Charles Bukowski steals my nerve.

Charles Bukowski slams the door.
His poetry rocks,
that's for damned sure.
I'm dead on the floor,
begging for more,
but Charles Bukowski slams the door.

Chattering Teeth Don't Gnash and Weep

(I'm perfecting the art of inane chatter while we wait.)
The water was so clear, the rocks were right there . . .

(Nothing matters anymore worth arguing about.)
Lucille's daughter's kitchen is being renovated . . .

(No need to inject reality into the mix.)
Once I lose my hair, I won't be playing bridge . . .

(Inanity alone won't fix mom's cancer . . .)
I had to hold the ladder, then we got a new one . . .

(. . . or make bearable the endless infusions.)
The girls always make such beautiful cookies . . .

(At least someone's blood pressure's in check.)
Remind me to bring in the hibiscus . . .

(The secret art of listening in silence eludes me.)
Lucille's artistic daughter, you know the one I mean . . .

Christmas List

(found poetry)

- Classical Electrodynamics: Jackson (3rd Edition)
- Classical Mechanics: Goldstein (3rd Edition)
- Advanced Condensed Matter Physics: Sander
- Condensed Matter Physics: Marder
- Fantasies of Flight
- Order out of Chaos
- Works by Plato
- The Renaissance: Walter Pater
- The Satanic Verses
- The Devil's Dictionary
- The Flowers of Evil
- Socks
- A book of piano solos by Rachmaninoff, Chopin, Mozart, or anyone good
- A drawing book of plain white paper
- A TI-Inspire Calculator (mine's broken)
- Rechargeable batteries and battery recharger

Clutching the History of My Rosary

I believed I would never clutch a rosary as my forebears had,
fervently praying, as they had been taught, for release from
the realities before their eyes. Is it true that a desperate human
being is willing to bend, in any direction, even toward lies and
chaos, as long as it is away from pain?

A rosary is flexible, a bunch of beads on a long string
in a circle, which you go around and around, holding each
bead in turn, praying the same prayers over and over until
your prayers are answered or until you've had enough praying.
I don't even know if I've got the process right. I never paid
enough attention to learn all of what I should believe. All
religious ideas, as explained to me as a child, appeared to be
absurd. No one believed them.

The last of the rosaries I called my own is one I'd bought
for myself. It was perfect.

It was all white. It glowed in the dark. I found it packaged
in plastic, hanging on a hook in a sacred store. It was the answer
to the need I never knew I had until the moment I saw it, in all
its promise glory. If I needed it at night when no one was
around to turn on the light, I would always be able to find it.
It was a reasonable way to fight back, in the night, against
the dark.

I knew owning a plastic, glow-in-the-dark rosary was
heresy. Girls held precious the rosaries passed down by their
grandmothers. How old was I, when I last believed I had control
of the universe? Circling the rosary, praying over and over
for things to be different.

Please, let things be different this time around!

I clutch the history of my rosary. How brave and foolish
and utterly human, to turn from pain to chaos, to clutch hope
and to try certainty.

To believe, to truly believe, the absurd.

Cobra

The cobra uncoils and stretches up, slips its head
from under the woven lid of its keeper's rattan basket
and slowly unsheathes its neck from its hood.

Balanced and poised, with a slight, weaving bob,
it senses its surroundings with chill eyes,
tastes the air with slitted, flitting tongue,
searches for life scents through odor-sensitive pores
dimpling reptilian skin.

It absorbs the scared sweats
of the stock-still creatures which surround it.
It takes it all in.

The splendor!
The world is full of possible prey.

It eyes the menu for today's feast.
All for the choosing.
None may resist.

It selects. It strikes. It dines.

Coming Out Dead

I'm planning a big farewell party
to tell everyone that I know
how lovely it is to be going,
though I'm not really ready to go.

I've wondered forever about this.
What's taking me down in the end?
I know I'll eventually be "death-kissed."
"Old Age" is my dearest new friend.

It's obvious to me and my loved ones,
I'm not quite the girl that I was.
I've been so forgetful, and then some,
but never knew what was the cause.

Rhyming this poem is easy.
I'm finding the words that I need
to tell you I've come down with something.
It will shorten the time I've to breathe.

You seriously don't want to join me!
This journey I've started is hard.
I'd rather be writing a story
or reading a play by the Bard.

I'll say it just once. Listen up, please.
My mind is a terrible mess.
What I've got is an awful condition.
I forget what it is. Help me guess?

Construction of the Poem

Selecting the proper set of letters to exquisitely express one's thoughts is like preparing a new recipe from scratch. Grow the fresh foodstuffs from seed. You know you're going to want apple pie; be sure to plant the apple tree three years ago. Examine one's word pantry. Check each staple for a use-by date. Go shopping if the right combinations are not found on the shelf.

What is finally ingested must be a work of art which sustains in the consumer the sense that there exists in the world a lunge towards beauty. A poem must not leave in its wake an enduring satisfaction or produce a sated feeling that never wanes. The aroma of a poem in the process of consumption must awaken an ever-harder-to-appease appetite. With each bite, it bestirs a more deeply felt, ravenous hunger.

The deliciousness of full immersion in a poem should generate an endless pang, a swooning grief, anticipation of the last word. The path to the end of a poem must elicit dread, the sense of loss that will fall over the soul when all is said.

How terrible, the realization: new knowledge that the poem, in all its fits and spasms, is decked out for final disaster. Silence looms!

It's doomed. Words will run out. The poem will, most certainly, end.

Cooperation Underground

In the dead of winter, under the snow, under this dirt in my garden, the roots of my neighbor's pines sing to the roots of my maple.

"On special today! Extra energy, free! Come, get'cher products of photosynthesis. Get them while they last!"

And, in the broad-leaf days of summer, my maple returns the favor.

"Here, we brought back that sugar we borrowed."

They don't fight over limited resources. They take what they need of the sun in the sky and the water underground and bank the bounty of their leaves. Excess production goes into a shared account, to be drawn by whoever needs it. They don't keep a running balance to see who gives more and who takes more. What's a little excess energy among photosynthesizing friends?

Deciduous and coniferous trees live patiently as neighbors and truly appreciate their differences. The process of seed formation that works for one is alien to the other. A neighboring tree's leaves are shaped differently and their flowers bloom at different times of the year, and these are cause for celebration. Each is working, in its own season. They cooperate, to mutual benefit. They share.

Are they running on chemistry alone?

It's my guess, the punch line to the funniest joke the other side of the sod is "Xylem up and phloem down!"

Cows Fly Overhead

Soft, brown Guernsey cows fly in rows overhead, unperturbed. On their tails, swing cats in tow. Broad, black, upside-down umbrellas overflow with terrified-cat sweat, but we will not be disembarking anytime soon. We sell jars of cat sweat for a dime. Crows and bats and pigs battle in this reeking slime. We shake them down.

Find a wooden shoe at a garage sale and paint it.

Give me no more dollar-fifty beer hidden in a paper bag, just rosé wine. Lay me on a bed of your softest pachysandra. Feed me grapes, one by one. Blow in my ear until my eyes are wide-opened. Take your time. Little white lies are all harmless, brittle, crimson cousins.

At dawn yesterday, I dried tears off the iron fence protecting our garden. It still feels a lot like deer hunting season. The stags prance absentmindedly through fallow and glen and climb trails winding around the mountains. Leis of lianas gather graces of violets, forget-me-nots, and Turgenev paperbacks. They sell leaves to street vendors who buy lost trinkets wholesale.

Creeping up the fading aluminum siding, one twining vine sports a boa of purple blossoms.

Walking the forest trail or hiding among the swarming bees, hairy, gray, eight-eyed spiders, who usually languish alone in their webs, despair of finding human nature in real humans. They bite people, and die, poisoned right back.

Dimples. Pure dimples! Mini-marshmallows line up on cobs of yellow corn and melt. I don't mind the copycats, but I really wish they'd bake on their own time and in their own Crock Pots.

The schoolmarm's cornmeal mush wants a bit of salt. Henry says, "Run with it!" Forget him. Add tears, for salt. Tears will do. To hell with cholesterol, add the damned bacon.

I presume prescient rain clouds would drop me a sweater before my mother says she's cold.

We're on the moon already. Just call it. Simon says, you've won.

Crow on Roof

From my window, I can see that crow.
It's always there,
prancing to and fro at dawn,
scooping tasty morsels from the lawn.

But today, it's perched up on the roof
across the street
above mom's bedroom window,
pretending it's Poe's raven
above that bedroom door
on Pallus' bust.

He's really loud,
upset,
speaking in a literary dialect
I'll never understand.

It sounds like he's crying
a death sentence,

"Nevermore!"
"Nevermore!"
"Nevermore!"

Cubism Ruins Your Day

The best thing about Cubism is how it rips the heads off
dead flowers, a process termed "dead-heading."
Every good poem is dead-headed right out of the gene pool.

A Picasso is worth millions, literally.
Check your attic. Fifty thousand works!

When I used to see Cubist art, my first thought was this:
"My grandmother isn't home."

L'oréal looks so cute with that little apostrophe,
hanging there like a wink.

Fifteen tons, and whaddya get?
College graduation and deeper in debt.

*

Finally, a Post-modern garbage truck we can all get behind.
But, I digress.

Schwa . . . the punctuation mark for all eternity.
Funny thing, it used to mean "water."

---

* 1. Stop here, put your pencils down!
   2. Drop your drawers. Drool.
   3. Roll your eyes and apologize.
   6. Do you want your fries with ketchup or in the same gender
as your nitty-gritty?
   5. Save your questions for your next wife.
   5:30. Wriggle out of that little black gnarl for me, Sugar.
   . Hold my beer.
          No, not you. Her.

Whaa?

Dada Fail

However hard I try, I make sense.

The words I ring around my Rosie mush lentils in June,
despite my huge horse.

So, ride me.

Ride me?
Hey, nonny, nonny . . . No!

Effin' I had a better window, my sans serif lyrics
would fling a coat over it.

Blend in, like pastels in the rain.

Sweet piranha-rich soil from Gretchen's Mill . . .how I raisined
over you! Curtailed all the minions . . .

Yet, loggy remains.

Smooth fries McFries.
With ketchup! Mmm . . .

Did you exist, but, somehow, I missed it?

Daddy Recites His Favorite Poem

"*There was a soldier . . .*in . . .

"*Algiers* it was . . . something about . . . *Foreign Legion* . . .
He was dying . . . someone . . . *took his hand.*"

A burst of confidence, and he snares most of the next line.
"*Tell my mother, I died . . . in a foreign land!*"

He grins.

Now, he continues.

Nothing.

Stymied, he repeats "foreign land," then forges on, to stumble
through the next part, where most of the words remain hidden.
". . . *mom . . . silver pear tree. . . .*"

He stops altogether. He's given up, utterly defeated.

"What else?" I prompt, with an eager smile.

Daddy remembers what he wants to tell me.

"I don't remember any more of the poem,
but I do remember, from the farm.
In the moonlight, pear tree leaves look like silver."

He beams at the memory. "They're beautiful!"

He looks up at me. He beams, brighter still.
"You're beautiful!"

Daytime. Am I Dreaming?

In pairs on the lawn on the first day of spring,
as I watch from my kitchen window,
giant pandas tango on piles of melting snow.

From the deck in my backyard,
I see six baby otters frolicking in the pond,
playing Keep Away with a beach ball.

I entice into a jar
a swarm of lightning bugs,
pay them a buck to paint my driveway neon green.

I crawl between the roots of the pom-pom tree
to spy on the fairies circling the Maypole.
They glow with delight.
They whirl with colored ribbons.
They stop. They kiss. They pop—invisible!

All these are more real to me
than seventeen dead
in the middle of the school day
on TV.

Dive Through the Ice!

said her heart. She always listened to her heart, so she raced
down the snowy pier, set her eyes on her mark in the lake,

and . . .

She
swam
out forty feet,   plunged . . .
faster than at her
high school swim meets,
and pushed her four-year-old
son's head up, through the frigid
water, and pushed his flailing body up
and over the side of the boat and into his father's
     arms. Her ears heard the boy splutter and cry. Her
          arms, too spent to hoist herself in her sodden clothes,
               clung to the side. Her legs dangled below. Her lips
                    skipped the lashing of her drunken husband,
                         but enunciated their address into his
                              cellphone as he rowed back to
                                   shore. Her heart grew
                                        heavy and

                                             .

                                             .

                                             s

                                             .

                                        a

                                             .

                                        .

. . . .   . k   .   .   . n   .

Do Not Marry a Poet

If I were a young girl,
my whole life ahead,
I'd not choose a poet.
I'd wed you instead.

There've been frosty mornings
when I'm scraping ice.
The kids missed the school bus.
I don't sound so nice.

The laundry's still wet,
the machine's on the fritz.
I've got no clean undies.
My sweatshirt's all ripped.

My friend's diagnosis
left her weepy and bald.
My iPhone's just died.
It's a mystery, who's called.

I'm in a great hurry,
have you seen my shoe?
The cat peed the carpet?!
I'm yelling. At you.

On mornings like this,
I might sound like a pain,
but it isn't a poet
who'll hear me complain.

Dragon Qi Gong

Once a year, I begin anew.

The promise:
I will become master of Dragon Qi Gong.

Such is the persuasive nature of determination.

I revel in delusion
at the annual birthday celebration
of long-dead Tai Chi Master Jou, Tsung Hwa.

Then, I return home.

The car door is not even shut
before the curling smoke fizzles.
The dragon, a misty memory, fades fast.
My sensei's breath, wasted on unrepentant ears.

I have offered my spark to others in attendance,
hopeful that Tai Chi teachers will return
to gather in this garden
for eons to come.

I wear the black-and-gold
Dragon Qi Gong
t-shirt
to bed.

Dragonfly

Hello, you little dragonfly,
   perched, calm, upon your leaf.
Are you aware how summer's sun gleams,
   radiates from your wings?

Adorable confection!
   Painted on your mirrored twins:
pearl-pink gems, platinum scrolls,
   and iridescent rims.

Pure sheers, in flight. You're wings!
   Delight!—entirely perfection.
I gaze, transfixed—translucent lace,
   your wings hold my attention.

If not for photographic craft,
   there's nothing more I'd mention.
In pictures, you've an abdomen
   with tough and wrinkled skin.

I stare, enraptured. You've appeared!—
   Grace, glistening in the light.
I hold my breath, anticipate
   your sudden lift to flight.

I plead for your devotion,
   but you're fickle as the wind.
You will not stay with me for life,
   though often I pretend.

You'll choose to leave, abandon me,
   though I'd cherish you forever.
You love the air, its buoyancy,
   how it lets you go—wherever.

Dreaming of Vaccination

What was it I was doing when I was interrupted
by fear for my life?

The last time I played my flute,
I had not felt the need to promise myself
I would play again.

New socks have arrived in cardboard,
which is not a great surface for sustaining a virus.

When my grandson left last weekend,
I did not remember to wash my hands.

I've forgotten why I cried, "I want to live!"
the day after the pandemic struck.

The weekend will be hot.
It would have been perfect
for dipping my toes in the ocean.

An octopus slithers in the silt near the shore
without releasing its ink.
I'd be happy to switch bodies.

O, Belmar Beach,
possibly overcrowded, and therefore possibly lethal,
I avoid the soothe of your silky sands.

But, here, eat my spirit, long distance!

I stand on my front porch
and toss my heart
into today's southeasterly winds.

Elements

Air

I am my thoughts. I am a student of what is and what could be.
I am reflection. I am too busy with observation, introspection,
analysis, judgment, and plans for the future to take any action
besides being myself, recording my thoughts.

Earth

I am a writer. My words reflect my thoughts.
If I am in luck, I will place my thoughts into the written record.
Take my thoughts and pass them on.
Record the thoughts you've created, triggered by
your absorbing and being consumed by my words.
What thoughts pop up in your own head as you swim deep,
deep in my thoughts, pondering my experience?
Become who I am. I have spent a lifetime becoming you.
Now, I am reflecting you. Reflect me. Reflect me.
Echo me. I still exist. I am my thoughts—now, in you.

Fire

Let it all not be to waste. Let it not continue exactly as it is now.
Throw the whole of it into the fire.
What's left, after the whole of it is gone to ashes, is precious.
The ashes become washed away in the oceans, eons of tears.
It is thoughts that remain. I am my thoughts.
Reflected in you, I am still here. I have become purified.

Wind

Let it all not continue exactly as it is now.
Let it matter that I was here.
Let my thoughts remain, in you.
Take time to reflect my thoughts, and I am here again.

Embracing the Bitter Present

If this winter storm is all there is, I embrace it.
I stand erect, my face turned skyward,
welcoming this biting sleet.
I feel the stinging on my nose,
my forehead, chin, and cheeks.
My eyes are shut. My eyelids burn.
I can't remember when today's assault began.

I dread each drip of melting ice
that's sliding down my neck.
It's stroking each and every inch of bared skin.
It reaches in under my clothing,
dropping icy fingers ever lower.
Cold creeps along trembling pathways
until each and every nerve is shaking.

I must endure, so I'll be here
for one more daffodil's eruption through the snow,
to puff and blow the fluffy strings
off one more dandelion,
and allow the juice of one more fleshly ripe peach
to dribble, luscious, down my chin.

I yearn for one more autumn,
another bath in crisp, yellow leaves.
Another campfire hearth to sing around.
To beg again, "S'more s'mores, please!"
To hear guitar strings, unused to strumming, twang.
To sing.

I grit my teeth and grin into the bitter wind,
as if the razor slash from this brash fight with winter,
which I must win, to live,
to live, to live, to live!
is the last thing, ever, I will feel.

Endless Optimism

At any time,
 I expect a turn--

from work
  boring
    thankless chore
  my hands
    raw
     skin scraped
       pink
           stinging with blisters
    bucket
  grimy
      grey water
         sunken gunk
           glistening slick
mop handle
        slimy
          wet stick wet
            wetstickystick
 the stench
the stench
 bleach

--the turn!

bliss
 champagne   bubbles
   laughing up my nose
     tickling
 my muse
   woozywith de   light
   the poem
     the poem
the poem
       the poem
               this poem

Falling

I'm falling as snow between pine needles.

I'm falling as a white-skirted tennis player on a first date with a seeded semi-pro who has already unwittingly revealed his Bobby Riggs attitude. I've been tumbling head-over-heels, having missed his ruthless first serve, then the second, and all the rest. We've reached the bottom of the ball bag. We were going to switch serves only after the server had lost a point. And, I had been so determined to Billie Jean King my way around my side of the net!

I'm falling out of step, like this saxophone player, stumbling, in front of me, on the football field at marching band practice. His mother made him sign up for after-school activities to keep him out of trouble because she's at home in bed in her sixth year of dying from a brain tumor.

I'm falling without being noticed, like the lacy pink edge of a slip falling below the hemline of the high school drop-out at her first secretarial job who doesn't realize until her lunch break that the shoulder strap of her slip is broken. Her new boss ripped the slip strap with his clumsy groping, his way of welcoming the new girl into the typing pool. She can't fix it until she gets home; yet, she finds she doesn't even care anymore about slips, or even modesty, not since Natalie Wood was found drowned in the same ocean where her husband's yacht was floating, with him aboard, asleep.

I'm falling as the swatted fly, disappearing into the patterned rug.

I'm falling as freely as the fledgling robin, confident my mother would never push me beyond my limitations and unaware that the last free worm I will ever know has already been slipped down my gullet.

I'm falling quickly, as sheets, torn from the clothesline, balled up and thrown into the wicker basket under the summer thunderstorm crashing, cashing in its nimbus chips.

I'm falling to the forest floor, a tree bashing the moss, bouncing to the cadence of ice dripping as last year's nests thaw and melt, pelting shriveled leaves still clinging to my lowest boughs.

Fighting Poetry Workshop "Rules"

I'm going to fight for my right to place commas
anywhere I like

                                    or to leave them out
                                        as I see fit.

            My poems will not look or feel "right."

Watch me bulldoze through **IAMBS**.

I rhyme when I want to
and skip a beat, here and there,
without a care as to whether I conform
to any particular type of poetic form.

Or not.

My poems reflect me.
I bring out a bare-naked, screaming poem more often
than one fully dressed, permed, powdered, hatted,
subdued
and ready for church.

            I try to make do,
        write traditional haiku
            using simple words.

Rats.
Once again, counting syllables, I've left out the season word.

First Symptom of the Fatal Brain Tumor

Ma girl tell me sop'em,
da damn winshielt wappers
jangelt en erk, erk, erk, erk.
Annit wad'hn't eden rainin', she set.

Erk, erk, erk,
jerkin' in jerkin',
en she turnt em off.
En dey wadn't eden ohn.

Maybe it wat dat tahm I dit dat met?
She wud askin'.

Mebbe, I said.
Yeah, prolly.

Dat wa eight years ago! she set.
Ah hain't touched it in eight years!

Yep, prolly dat, I set.

I never touched it, I addit.

Yo smart, she set.

Nop, I set.
Welp, maybe, I set.
Huh, musta bin funny, eh?

Nop, she set.
Uh, nop! Not funny.

She dai now.

Flying Cars and Pickle Jars

Drones for ordinary citizens are illegal here, but the law is not enforced. Schools for skeet shooting offer graduate degrees in defensive droning. They rubber-stamped me a phony drone license.

My kids have the option of having perfect children, clones of themselves and their siblings, but they are unaware of their own perfection. They don't believe me when I tell them how lucky a mom I am. They don't listen when I tell them: Wait! Technology will catch up.

I bought a self-flying sports car, a Muskette. I'm an official Musketeer.

My favorite pickles come in a glass jar with an old-fashioned vacuum-sealed lid. The gym promises I'll be able to open a pickle jar after one month of personal training or I can get my money back.

I just bet our retirement account on tech-connected wearables with built-in personal defense systems. The products, under two brand names, "Drone-Away!" and "Perimeter," are both sold with money-back guarantees.

For Six-Year-Old Emily

I put a bottle of Stewart's Birch Beer on the dining table
next to the Orange Fanta and the box of colored plastic straws.

Emily remembers!

"My father fell down off the kitchen chair," says Emily.

My six-year-old daughter is not listening.
Her brow is furrowed, contemplating her birthday wish.

"We had spaghetti for dinner."

"And he could not walk."

"Then he got in his car and had an accident."

The wax is melting into the icing.

"So, I will never drink beer!" says Emily happily.
Triumphant, she tosses her gossamer curls.

"It runs in my family." She giggles.
So proud of herself, Emily smiles broadly.

I add my own silent wish.

My daughter blows out the candles.

I palm the bottle of Stewart's Birch Beer, make it disappear.
I sidle over to the refrigerator and lay it down inside,
tuck it behind the eggs on the lower shelf.

When I cut the cake, I don't ask, "Who wants soda?"
Instead, I pour out six small paper cups of Orange Fanta.

I say, "What color straw do you want?"
and let them pick their own.

Forgotten

I walk from my car to the edge of the forest. I yearn to enter, to explore. But, I fear, I am already lost. I'd never find my way in and back out again. I've been forgotten by the woods. There's a mist of fear hovering in there. Birds sing to each other, but they don't even remember who I am.

I sit on the curb, next to the hot car, in the hot sun, and eat my ham and swiss. The parking lot reeks of the mechanical world. It smells of old tires and gasoline. It echoes with the silent screeches of spent youths cheering burning rubber and the unhooking of bra cups.

Of a spilled Big Gulp, all that remains is a brown smear on the tar, a plastic lid and straw, and a small gathering of once-ecstatic, now dead, bees. Waxed paper cups haven't been found anywhere around here in years, and the plastic one with the logo that held the icy cold treat is not here, not anywhere that I can see.

The cool of the forest floor mocks me with its indifference, mocks and mocks, drones on and on and on. It insists I admit the truth—that I am not in there.

But, I realize, I am not sure I'm in *here,* either, not inside my own body. All I know is, I am lost.

I close my eyes, shed my human skin, and float into my imagination. But, it cannot compare. It cannot hold these memories of cool forest forever.

My tears evaporate, heated on the pavement. My head is bent, as if in prayer, facing the sticky, stinky tar. Is this, now, how it is? This is the only human environment?

It is not humane. It doesn't know how to caress. It can't soothe, and I've forgotten where else there is that I can go. Where do I even go to, when I want to go home?

Four Water Poems for Soldiers of WWI

A Call to Arms

On the shore of the Mogami,
wakened by the roar of the river,
a single dewdrop,
scolded, shaken,
scootches on down his leaf's stem
and hastens toward the roiling sea.

All Europe Joins the Conflagration

Released dewdrops drop,
ride growing streams,
rush to Mogami River.

Americans Declare War

The call of the mighty Mogami
excites the last, tiny dewdrop
to leap from his cozy leaf
and join his band of brothers,
cascading, on their rivulets,
towards the roaring,
tumultuous ocean.

Memorial Day Haiku

Drops gather, as clouds,
drift in, this summer weekend,
storm the Jersey Shore.

Glass Slippers

As I explored my path through life, I'd no idea how worn
the ground beneath my feet, nor how easily I'd been led
to choose the options I'd selected, believing the choices
were mine, made freely.

Hidden worlds lay just beyond the shield, camouflage
prepared before I breathed. Glass slippers had been custom-
made for my uncalloused feet.

The winding road—I thought I'd picked—pre-carved,
from rough terrain. Streamlined and smoothed. Made mossy,
by design. It was designed for me.

My folks, both models of restraint, gave me my voice,
encouraged me to think, fed me hope I'd visit places they'd
only longed to see.

I am an artist. Do I dabble exclusively in hues I've found
laid out, already on my palette? Isn't imagination invented
by you and me?

My children dance and trip in pretty shoes. I see, they're
also made of glass, unsuitable for straying from the beaten
path, not fit for those who would explore.

In shoes like those, they'll never see much more than
what I saw, where I went; no lands or worlds or things
beyond my shore.

Haiku Under an Autumn Moon

To rake, or not to . . .
No! How often does a lawn
glisten gold at dawn?

Pen poised for capture.
October full moon lingers
while I gaze, transfixed.

Shiny, glimmering,
slippery with leaves, gilt porch
gleams in autumn sun.

Promised, the first snow!
My husband mows. Finally,
our lawn's last haircut.

Strung along dead limbs,
freshly yellowed leaves, not crisped.
Sepia kicks in.

Hours in darkness.
Your pillow, empty. Mine, wet.
No sounds. None at all.

His Throat Had Been Closing

I was notified through an email list.

> *His throat had been closing for the past five weeks,*
> *so essentially, he starved to death*

this man I never knew, writes someone I never knew,
who reports they were told this news by the man's wife,
another person I never knew.

There are no links to click on in this email
from this email list I don't recognize.

The news of his death, of his suffering,
of his throat closing, closing,
saddens me as, at the same time, it brings me closer
to these people I never knew.

I am grateful for the chance to lessen their grief,
if it does, in fact, lessen their grief to share it with me,
this person they never knew, who still, once a month,
checks her original email account.

I am everyone's mommy in this online garden, the net.

mommy@garden.net

Home Schooled

Guppies living in a tank,
for nowhere else to swim,
don't contemplate escaping.
There's no way out. Or in.

Adults will eat their Guppy Chow
and eat their babies, too.
A human hand must net the tots,
remove them from the pool.

In nature, who will play the save?
A plant. A lucky nook.
A place to hide. A rock below.
Do guppies even look?

If a guppy stays intact,
a guppy mate he'll seek.
Guppy babies look delish!
Mmm, what a dainty treat!

Nowhere else I'd wish to go,
no place I'd rather be.
Ah, simple fare and simple joy.
The guppy life for me!

How a Marine Felt When He Left Kuwait

It's a great feeling!

—an old TV commercial for Pearl Drops Tooth Polish

"I left Kuwait. It was a great feeling. To be alive,"
was posted on social media by a soldier
whose companions did not all make it.

I read those words, "a great feeling."

"A great feeling."
I thought I had heard the same phrase somewhere before.
I flashed back to an old TV commercial
for a smile-whitening, breath-freshening toothpaste.

The close-up of a mouth.
The tongue, sliding across a row of gleaming white teeth.
A satisfied smugness in the voice.

"It's a great feeling! Pearl Drops Tooth Polish."

No.
Not. The. Same.
Definitely, no.

I was mistaken! Nothing was the same.

Words. Words have no meaning. None, at all.

How Close I Was

(after Emily Dickinson)

How close I was !

—to kisses,
to sharing lips

Touch!
—Is that asking
too much?

The rulebooks
are wrong!!

My song—in your throat
echoes the glee,

your hand—
traveling up—

—my knee.

How Did Jackson Pollock Know When a Painting Was Done?

Pollock's paint poured and dripped so splashedly, dastardly spilling, spitting the virginity off the canvas. The wall was broken. But, where in Pollock's book of *Art Rules* was it? What told him?

"When!"

When was it time to do it? To end it?

"Put down your bucket!"
"Say, 'Fuck it!'"
"Ignore the other half-filled buckets still on the floor!"
"Don't rush out the door to buy more paint!"
"Stop! You're there. Take a walk. Get some air, sir."

Was there ever a line Jackson Pollock didn't cross?

Or, did Pollock simply gauge whether there was enough time for the paint already on the canvas on the floor to dry before the dealer came to pick it up and take it to the buyer?

Did Pollock ever try to save some paint for later?

Or, was the work, when he stopped, always—

"Done!"
"A task complete!"
"The last drop, dolloped just right!"

He *knew*. It was time to quit for the night and go home.

Did he follow rules? What rules? Is it art?

How did Jackson Pollock know when a painting was done?

How Haiku Saved My Life

Was something burning?

You wondered what you'd left on the stove.

Then, you saw flames at your elbow. FIRE! FIRE! FIRE! FIRE! THE COUCH IS ON FIRE! FIRE! FIRE!

You batted the green leather couch, smacked it with your fist, twice, three times, four. Battled the fire-breathing dragon. And you channeled Smokey, the Bear, drowning the campfire out—three times—as you poured your glassful of water into the smoldering pinhole.

The smoke detector had not gone off. The puppy remained asleep on the floor at your feet in his sunbeam.

A lingering wisp of smoke curled up from the couch to where your son slept in his bed in the loft. He'd merely mumbled a bit.

"Fire? Huh, wha-huh?... zzz..."

He promptly went back to sleep.

His twin brother was still sound asleep in the basement.

His little sister was still sound asleep upstairs in her bedroom with her door shut.

You had almost just gotten into the shower.

You'd stopped, to write yet another haiku, as usual.

If you hadn't had a haiku crooning to you, needling you to write it, right away, you would have had shampoo in your eyes and taken an extra few seconds to rinse off, towel dry, and wonder who was already up, making bacon, making the smoke detector go off on a weekend. FLAMES! FLAMES! FLAMES! FLAMES! FLAMES! FLAMES!

Your whole life as you know it would have been over.

And it wasn't, because of haiku.

After you put out the tiny fire, you repositioned that makeup mirror, the one your daughter had left on the table next to the picture window—so it wouldn't catch any more sunlight and concentrate its reflection onto the leather couch, where its intense focus might start a little fire and FIRE YOU UP! WAKE YOU UP TO YOUR LIFE!

How to Watch Your Mother Die

Buddha.
Big Bang.
Pow!

Separate, into three: your origin, yourself, and your destiny.

Realize, this is going to take a while. Be patient.
Open her cans.

Don't quibble.
Unless you've always wanted to. Now's your chance.

To love is to act.
Find an appropriate costume for each scene.
Let your mother be the Pope in her dreams.

There is strength in numbers.
You are more than one person,
you are connected to your mother.

Grant her every deathbed wish.

Love her enough, and the universe will implode.
Her father will be a doctor and bring his daughter
into his practice. They will save each other's lives.

Apologize for every moment her heart sank
because you were you and not her, every time
she felt kicked in her stomach—you had to kick your way out,
to get past her curfew … but don't complain.

After she's gone, re-create your mother in your mind.
Explain to her what you meant when you said,
"The Blue Screen of Death."

Now, she can't hear you.
Now, she can't argue, and neither can you.

How to Write Free Verse

CONTENT

Words, whether they make sense or not.
Punctuation optional.

FORM

Any number of lines and blanks.
Any formatting.
Any nonsense.
No arguments. (Argument? See: "How to Write Drivel.")

ACCEPTABLE

Smarm.
Sarcasm.
Crap.
Facts. It's irrelevant whether anyone believes them.
Comment on society, humanity, my failings.
Picture words? Okay.
Can be very long. Or, just one word. Or none.

THEME

Meaningful, even if only to Author.
Memorable, even if only to Author.

I Am Fire

I am fire today.

You!
Water?
Keep your distance.
I've got designs, dibs on the day.

Wet, lissome wishes?
You, I will ignore.

Boggy, poolish eyes and languid kisses?
You and yours, I will steam, sizzle, vaporize, and destroy!

You, over there!
You, with the dried tear streaks
and crisp leaves and twigs,
twisted, intertwined in your matted hair.
Are you feeling . . . flammable?

Come, be fuel to my fire!
Let us revel in the night.
Share my heat.
Be my delight.

Come close.

Closer.

I need someone. Now!
Someone to ignite.

I Dared to Leave Footprints

Your free will heightens the effervescence of your smile. Oysters shed pearls on the waves for you. Mosquitoes cease their biting. Moths, lining the night with rage, fly into torchieres.

I weeded your gardens for you, though I did not understand what a flower was. I wept in delight at aromas I smelled for the first time.

You held my enemies at bay. You gifted me your striding shadow.

I dared to leave home with you in the dark. You had me smash fireflies underfoot to leave a glowing trail. But, I discovered, firefly light does not linger much longer than the bug.

I crept aboard your yacht to steal a fresh pen and notebook, and I caught you yawning at the view.

You had never agreed that "you" were one of the two in "us." I worried—I might be left fettered in a dungeon, stranded atop a snowy mountain, or entrapped in an endless maze.

I kissed the empty space between your poisoned lips, the last place I'd expected you to leave me. You were not there.

Once, on a moonless night, our oars held aloft by the love song of nesting grackles, we drifted to the brink of a waterfall. Mutual attraction predicted the inevitable disaster.

You left me for dead beneath the banyan tree we'd promised our younger selves we'd visit. Friends assumed you'd drowned in white paper, writing me love letters.

The tree still stands.

I Don't Want to Live Where They Have Live Trollops on Speed Dial

I watch the crows bowing and scraping to the majesty of
a spring day. At the lowest point in their bend, there it is:
a worm, or perhaps a crunchy morsel, in the midst of the dew.
A crow doesn't have to stretch to get at its treat, it just prances
and preens, opens its beak, and inhales. Then, it takes off.
The bugs it missed laugh in relief.

I want to be just like a crow, but I don't think I could do
the macarena without a net anymore.

My hairdresser's curls bounce. I want them, badly, on
my own head. I saw them on TV, happily intoxicated,
jumping on a trampoline. They looked relaxed. Were they
wasted, high on Lemon Up Creme Rinse?

I strode into the beauty parlor, all Jersey-girl frumpy-like,
buying promises like it was Saturday night in Manhattan.
A perm said, "You want me! You're so damn hot!"

I was a twenty-something who suddenly realized she
might get old and fat. I was afraid I'd turn out like my short-
haired cat, fond of swinging my gut girdle in front of the TV.
I was too young to know I could stop caring because nobody
cares.

I seriously doubt the climate has my back. As you may
have heard, I'm not moving to Vegas. You know what they
have there? Live trollops on speed dial.

The world will spin dry without me taking my mother's
advice, and she will blame me. Nothing has changed. Water
hydrants still spill their guts. Frogs escape ponds. You are
cawing, screeching again, hurting my ears like it's 1945 and
war's over.

My eye hurts.

No, it doesn't! Stop believing me, just love my lies.

I Hate the New Kid on the Writer's Block!

My characters like to play Freeze Tag.
They might be in mid-stride, then suddenly balk.

Now, I can't make them giggle.
I can't make them fall.
They refuse to laugh.
Won't move.
Won't talk.
Not at all.
It's a child's game, I see.
A good joke, on me.

As they wait to be set free, they stand firm.
They won't hover or tremble or wiggle or squirm.
They won't move a thing, like the game's not begun.
They just wait for the tap, for the signal to run.

But, I am not "It."
It's not *me* they obey.

This inane game of Freeze Tag might go on all day.
I watch them.
All poised, they see their next step.
But, refusing to take it, they whisper, "Not yet!"
We wait.

Till the Muse makes her rounds, sets them free.
She'll touch each one's shoulder.
They'll run home . . . to me!

I Love My Thickening Waist

My younger sister complained my body looked odd.
Despite my underwire bra, my breasts sagged.

They were "not in the right place."
She wanted me to go shopping with her.

She promised, the new-fangled bra-engineering
asks the minimum in additional constricting.

I refused to consider high-tech breast interventions.
I did not need a solution to my "problem."

Years later, my sister fell in love with her own fallen breasts.
Her arrival at self-acceptance astonished her.

Our 102-year-old grandmother had gorgeous breasts.
One was growing a lump, the first stages of cancer.

After her sponge bath, I was getting her dressed
and she shared with me a trick she'd discovered.

We tucked her long, skinny, wobbly breasts
into the elastic waistband of her panties.

I Married a Mystery

If we had gone on our honeymoon to Hawaii for a week,
I'd have spent the whole time racking my brains,
tearing my hair out, trying to think of something fun
we could do together.

I'd say, "How about, let's go to a luau!"

He'd say, "I don't think I'd like that kind of food
and I don't think I've ever heard that kind of music
and I'm not in the mood to go out. But, you can go.
I'll stay in the hotel and watch TV."

Love is strange, and relationship does not always
have to involve event tickets.

We did see a Broadway show.
Once, when we were dating.

But, when we got home after the wedding ceremony,
my husband said, "Finally! I can take off the mask!"

I thought I was the only one wearing a veil
on that trip down the aisle.

So, who did I marry?

I Read and I Write

I wake and exercise in bed every morning
to get the blood flowing
so as not to pull a muscle when I breathe.

I take inventory.
I make sure I'm inhaling.
Exhaling, too.

Even still, I make mistakes.
I put down a foot that's still asleep.
Answer the phone before I'm awake.

I read and I write as fast as I can.
Who knows when this electronic ink will dry up?
There's so much more to learn, to know, to share.

Too soon, I'll die.
All this prep work will have been in vain:
this reading, this writing, this connecting the dots.

Unless *you* pick up the pieces.
Take up this crazy quilt I've started
and add on.

I Still Carry Wendy's Troll

I listen to the constant beep, booping.

" . . beep . . . . beep . . . . beep . . . Boooop! . . . . beep . . . "

There is a misty memory hovering in the smell of the fake-
flower scent of the industrial-strength disinfectant.

As I study the glowing numbers and the flashing lights at the
foot of my father's hospital bed, I vividly recall the brilliance
of the shine in my father's eyes as he handed me some lilac
cuttings to take with us to our first apartment.

I'd remarked, then, on how strong they smelled.

The smell will last, he said. That's the great thing about lilacs.
Put them in water right away, and it will smell like home
for a very long time. I gave you a lot, so you can plant some.
They'll take root. They'll come back every year.

I hated the stench of lilac, but I smiled. I was willing to suffer
in silence for the hour-and-a-half trip home so we could replant
them where Dad would see them every time he'd come to visit.

But the huge bunch of the flowers he'd given us overwhelmed
us in our tiny Toyota. We'd had to stop at the side of the road
and throw them out just so my husband could stop sneezing.
I was happy to be able to breathe freely again.

I recall how I'd brushed, with my fingertips, my friend Wendy's
ugly troll's blue nylon hair. Its phosphorescence shimmered
in the sunlight at the playground. Yet, it's brilliance was
eclipsed by Wendy's essential smile.

> *The physical claim,*
> *tangential*
> *to the sublime.*

I Wake Up Tingling

In anticipation of my husband's touching, I used to wake
up tingling, eager and ready to spring alive. Later, I'd skip
out of bed and dance down the hall, even before my kids
started calling "Mom!"

Now, I'm falling out of bed, tripping over my own feet,
and reeling, simply standing. Soon, I might not be typing
at all. When will computers expect my words aloud—just as
this old tongue becomes glued? When my lungs fight for air,
how will I make myself clear?

Computers may not understand how I compile my thoughts
into verbs and nouns and tosses of my head, nor glean meaning
from that sidelong smile I do that says, in shorthand, "I love
you, and I'm grateful for the zillion things you do. Like this
morning, when you cleared the snow off my car, brought in
the mail and newspaper, made coffee and oatmeal for two
with fresh blueberries and bacon, and you left for work
to bring home the bacon for our future. You do this for me,
for us, every morning, whether I'm up already or not."

If, someday, I can't type or talk, I might sit and smile
when I need to show you my heart. I might grimace, trying
my best to be there for you.

But, these tingling fingers and arms, at one in the morning,
give me alarm.

If, someday, I'm incommunicado and you're not here
with me to listen and share my desires, my hopes and my
dreams, with the world, who will know what I need?

A computer can't read what's inside my brain.

Who knows me as well as you do?

Who will see when I'm in pain?

Who will care who I am or know what I like?

Who is it, who will grin at my smile, long after its passing,
and, having understood, will remember that they, too, once,
had found someone like you?

If You See Yourself in These Three Poems, "Poof!"

I. Wait For It

We sat butt cheek to butt cheek on the concrete wall by the church. The one pen we owned lacked sufficient ink to write a check. The waterfowl on the pond in the public park showed not the slightest interest in contempt of court.

"Bolivia is colder," they sang. Even the frogs knew how to get to Bolivia. We lived to gather imagery for novels we wouldn't write. We erected tombstones for our descendants.

II. Star-Crossed

I still see stars from being sucker-punched with your visions. You dished *Casablanca*, "Nighthawks at the Diner," *No Exit*, "The Angels Want to Wear My Red Shoes," *On the Road*, *Harold and Maude*, and your own slick rendition of Ramesses II. You studied Fellini's *Satyricon*, Waters's *Pink Flamingos*, Bogart, Bette Davis, de Sade, and the ashes of Pompeii.

"I'm Spartacus!" you volunteered.

"We who are about to die, salute you!" I read aloud, with due diligence, as instructed.

"Get thee to Goshen!" you commanded, in your best pharaoh voice.

But the memory of her eyes refused to stay "Begone!"

III. I Will Be Writing More About You, and More Lies

The last game you taught me was Don't Exist. Before you'd ever met me, you'd made up the two rules:

1. You are not a reality in my universe.
2. I am not a reality in your universe.

When I heard you tell me you were ready to play Don't Exist with me, I felt swallowed whole, subsumed in lava.

Wait, what? Are you sure this is the only way you can keep breathing?

Then, I remembered: we play chess. The end game is all.

This is the last of my poems in which you will ever appear. Poof!

I'm Not Playing Bridge Anymore

Tying down a list of pleasant things to do is harder, now that
playing bridge is off the table. Reading, too, is not the enjoyable
pastime I once knew. Now, there's no reading, no chatting, and
nothing much else to do.

It always seemed rude to play on one's phone, since chatting
was fun. Would anyone care if I stared at my screen? Do they
know I constantly look, all around, everywhere, searching for
problems to borrow?

The poems I write while engaged with this phone,
I pretend are my answers to writings by strangers who waste
time online with me, fighting this stranger they can't see,
ruthlessly engaged in a lost, futile battle.

Yes, I see. This meter is stilted, this poem pathetic, yet
somehow inviting and full of tomatoes and much other
nonsense. There's chemical knowledge and preaching
by beagles.

Who says there's no purpose to randomization? I've filled
up three minutes with useful pretending.

My mother's impending demise isn't likely to happen until
I am beaten quite into submission, forgetting the rest of the
things I've been meaning to do. I'm thankful for poetry, lines
filled with nonsense. These poetic scribblings are easily
discarded, and will be, once happier days take the place of
poetic exams. I'll put on a simpering smile of amusement,
right dead in the center of all I've been hiding.

Amazing what nonsense can do! Another four minutes!

Forgetting the end of the world isn't magic, but real and
invisible, happening right now, and long overdue.

I might take to napping. It worked for my dad. Got him
through.

And now, with my mom, I could take up phonetics,
linguistics, or octaves.

I'd rather go sailing or eat dripping peaches or breed runt
chihuahuas. But, thinking of nonsense—instead of this losing,
this internal screaming, the stuff that I do in my battle with you?

This nonsense is better.

It's fine. It will just have to do.

I'm Taking a Texas Drawl With Me to Heaven

When I die someday and leave this world,
and I'm waiting to learn my fate,
I'll be pleading my case with a Texas drawl
as I reach that pearly gate.

I'll be asking good old Saint Peter,
"If you don't mind, check around.
Do you hear a girl, talks just like this?
She'll vouch for me, if she's around."

Gonna sit right next to Jesus,
if He'll let me get that close.
On my other side, I hope to find
that good ol' Holy Ghost.

Who am I kidding? I'm not going up.
I know just where I will be.
And, I'm not just one: there's three of us,
Leilani, Melene, and me.

We're never going to get into heaven.
But, heck, no, we don't care.
Where we're going, it's exciting!
They're reading poetry down there.

In Your Poem

I didn't know, I didn't know birds
until I heard the tanager across the lake
calling, calling across the lake
inside your poem.

And, now,
I am the bird's faithful listener.

He's singing!

My heart.
My breath, his sweet music.
I read and reread and reread
your poem.

I didn't know birds write poems.
Their words trill on human tongues.

I drink in my tanager.

I'm captive,
his voice calling, calling across the lake,
trilling, tanager music, thrilling on your tongue.

It's Spring, The Bumblebees Are Back

Yellow fluff balls bounce from blossom to blossom
on my purple-blooming bushes.

As a bumblebee touches down, it perks up and scurries
in a lusty frenzy, over and under and around each flower.

Its pointy, little, black stick legs are perfectly coordinated,
a ballerina en pointe on stage.

"The Dance of the Sugarplum Fairy,"
professionally choreographed.

Opening night, and I'm a toddler with his Nana
at my first Christmas show ever.

The dance steps, on blossom after blossom.
A TikTok gone viral.

Covered in pollen, on the other side of my picture window,
the dancing bumblebees are unaware of me.

So, why don't I go outside and join them?
It's not just that I fear bee stings.

It's that I'm tied to a keyboard.
But, my fingers are doing that same happy dance.

Measure out the lengths of growing color.

Increasing rays of beauteous sunlight.

Steady stream of musical melody.

Keeping rhythmic cadence.

Possibilities blossoming.

Tweets and thrills.

Brand new day.

Refreshed.

Joy

!

July

Ding, dong!

June rings, and I don't answer yet.

Ding, dong!

July! Come on in!

Summer sweeps clean dreary December's dead promises,
"I'm gonna be so darned diet good. My teeny-weeny yellow
bikini will fit me, come July!"

Summer was made for Tequila Sunrises, skinny dipping in the
Shenandoah, and corn stuck all up in your teeth.

Hot days say, "Scratch that sunburnt itch!"

Resistance to Dairy Queen melts on the patio.

July brings a symphony of farm-fresh flavors: watermelon,
cantaloupe, tomato, lettuce, radish, turnip, zucchini, cool, crisp
cucumber, and my favorite, peach . . .

Ah, fresh peaches!

Ah, peach pie with flaky, homemade crust!

Peach juice dribbling down my chin!

Strings of peach flesh tease my gums. Peach delight lingers.

I lick my fingers.

Kneading

Twist.
Press.
Wrap.
Smile.

Sniff, pull, push.
Buy the butter.
Dream the knife.
Slice the crust.

The wood cutting board scrolls past crisp crumbs.
Serrated points scrape across my soft palms.

Calloused dreams.

Spritz, steam.
Spritz, steam.
Spritz, steam.

Mushrooms mush neatly between two rows of ivories.
Flavor lassos French onion soup's stringy pull.

Beer in brown bags holds our seats
along the cold stone wall.

We watch.
Scores of policemen
enforce labor laws
prohibiting idleness
among the unemployable.

Those resting might have been better employed
if there was somewhere better to be,
better than where they belonged.

Lashed

A dead fly, stuck fast in a spider web in my bedroom
window screen these past many years, keeps me company.
I am comforted, knowing his wings don't beat. He hasn't
left, won't desert me.

The sight hasn't prompted me to brush his corpse free from
its lash. If I'd touch it, the desiccated body would fall apart.
I'd sweep up his crusty, dusty bits, deliver him to the trash
can, and carry the can to the curb.

Every Monday night, I consider it. Every Tuesday morning,
I hear the garbage truck, hear the metal cans clinking,
dropped on the street. My dead fly is still here. I haven't
done it, again.

I ask, again and again, why must you linger, dead fly?
Why torment me with your continued presence?

Why do I keep alive the mystery of why you arrived
to be with me?

When will this companion of mine, already fallen victim
to death and decay, finally drop off my screen? No longer
intact, His Brittleness will finally come apart, enough to
free himself and leave me.

I'm waiting to be rescued by time and gravity, but I don't
do a thing to hurry it along. I'm sure I'll miss his dry-fly,
gutless, faithful, soulless stare and silent song.

Life Is Not Easy

Take the responsibility train and don't get off where most
others do. It will keep going, beyond where you've been.
Soon, the train will stop and all the people will get off.

Except for a few. And, more will get on, and squeeze
in, and the car will fill. You'll have to stand or people
will sit on you. You'll feel mashed, and you'll struggle to
breathe. All will be squirming and giggling and moaning
and screaming, and the train will go faster and faster and
shake—shake violently. You'll go all queasy. Someone near you
will cry hysterically, "We're all going to die!" You'll hang onto
the shoulders in front of you, for dear life.

You'll feel like you're falling.

Then suddenly, the shaking will stop, the violence will
be over. But now, you're sailing forward, arcing downward.

Falling.

You look over the head of the woman at your side,
who's finally calming down. The scenery is flying by.
A line of trees. Rocks. The shore.

Your train is now facing straight down. Down, down,
down you fall, and you are floating in free fall, but have not
lost your balance. People are leaning against one another,
lined up in rows, like sardines in a can. The train is falling,
headed straight down, streaming. The passengers have all
laid down on the floor. They're quieted. Calm.

And, you notice, something has changed. They all
now appear to be strangely furry. You recognize, they are
lemmings. You are now a lemming. All are lemmings.

The rush to the sea floods your entire being with intense
heat. As you sink into the crowd and the train plunges into
the brine, and the salt and the drench and the seaweed and
fish whirl in around you and whip your head, your breath,
your eyes, your teeth, your knees—your nose starts to fill
with snails.

They wriggle inside you, and leave behind a line of
gooey slime. You feel the wetness. The coy, the balm. All
over you. Your whole body, inside and out. You're glad for
the cooling, especially of your feet. It's such a relief.

Life Without Father

My daughter named her kitchen, "No Man's Land," taking pride in her independence. She learned family recipes from her father and can create traditional dishes without help.

Her father learned family recipes from his father.

Where there were no hospitals, women died giving birth. Men who knew the secrets of the hearth could sustain their families.

At times when there was not enough meat, the girls in the family went without. My mother-in-law and sisters-in-law had nothing but rice. They are very much shorter than the men in the family.

When my father-in-law's father was disappeared, his son recreated his father's scent in his blackened wok.

Great-grandmother sent us his last, unfinished painting. It lies rolled up in a cardboard mailing tube, cradling cracked, brittle slivers—sharp, dried sticks of paint.

In the silenced years, it snowed in the mountains where no one lives. Though no one has seen it, it snows there every year.

My self-sufficient daughter's children wait to be conceived and born. They have yet to find a father.

Line Up Next to the Goal Line

"I know, I will win this race!"
She loved to run. Just like me! I run track.

"Run slower, don't beat all the boys."
The girls weren't trying to win? Why not?

"Your reputation was almost ruined!"
How do you explain a great-aunt's diary?

"Stick to croquet and needlepoint."
I thought that was only in the Dark Ages!

"Boys and brassieres will come later."
Run slower, so boys will like you? Sex ed, 1959?!

"Just be a smart lady."

Misogyny is crazy. But, how do you describe how insane it
really was? How much it hurts, to know how you were raised,
one in a long line of otherwise intelligent people, people who
were all forced to play along to survive in a misogynistic
society, forced to normalize the crazy.

But not me. I ran with my fourth grade class in a big circle
around the entire perimeter of the playground in a race to
determine the fastest runner in our class. Everyone seemed to
expect a boy would win. The boys ran their fastest. The girls
dawdled. Except for me. It never occurred to me to run slow.
I ran my damned fastest. I loved to run. And win.

A boy came in first and I came in second. But the class gathered
around we two winners and encouraged him to "Catch her! Kiss
her!" and he did run up to me from behind and squeezed me,
held me in a bear hug until the chanting became so frenzied, he
dropped me, from embarrassment.

I was baffled. Yet excited, and still out of breath.

LP

Side 1

I cannot help but to stop and smell the roses.
I love my neighbor as I love myself.
I brush and floss after every meal.
I pray the rosary daily after mass.
I look before I leap.
I mind my p's and q's.
I respect my elders.
I sing, oh, so sweetly.
I think sober thoughts and dream sweet dreams.
I leave well enough alone.
I am growing quite old and very, very wrinkled.

Side 2

I've got a tattoo.
I throw away the manual.
I catch the rainbow.
I fall in and sound off by twos.
I flirt, more than a little (actually, quite a lot).
I go for broke.
I dance naked on tables.
I drive a Ferrari I've "borrowed" without permission.
I do ALL things (in moderation, of course).
I wear nine-inch heels.
I laugh when they tell me, it's time for bed.

Lumps in Grandmother Devlin's Homemade Jam

I would take a spoonful of my grandmother's homemade
jam made with my grandfather's homegrown peaches and
spread it with a butter knife over my slice of toast, mashing
the lumps best I could without squishing the bread.

I'd brush off the uneatable hard peach lumps with the knife
onto the side of my plate, then smooth out what was left of the
jam so that every bite of toast would have the same exquisite
mouthfeel.

The first peach lump, I discovered when my grandmother
served me the first breakfast of my first sleepover away from
home when I was five.

Today, I would eat every lump in her jam, savor every
bump, revel in the unevenness of the flesh of peaches, cherish
the entire experience of peach jamnity, and cry, even wail to the
heavens, after I'd swallowed the final bit.

But I don't regret having discarded the lumps at the time,
when fresh jam from my grandmother's kitchen, made from my
grandfather's homegrown fruit, was divinity without end.

Lust for Life

I love Life.
I lust for Life.
I fox Life, intoxicate him. Wow him!

But, they say, Life is a jealous lover.
Once you've been taken by Death,
Life leaves you forevermore.

I'll be Death's conquest, that's for sure.
How could I, alone, not yield
to his irresistible touch?

When Death comes to court,
and woos,
and I stupidly give in,

I'll demand to see proof
—his unending devotion—
or I'll show him the door!

Will Life take me back?

I hope I'm not the type of girl
Death pesters forever.

I hope Life loves me more.

Making Do With a Dead Poem

This is a dead bird of a poem, and I am a cat, proudly dropping the carcass on your doorstep. This golden feather hat trilled and warbled, "Territt, twee-eet!"

It flew low, just out of my reach. But, my leap!

It's so much fun, showing you this dead thing I won!

It looked much cooler in flight. An Egyptian mummy, rising. The Halloween moon. Swaying daffodils.

It still has colors: orange, black ... it's a little dusty ....

But, it doesn't move anymore. Or, flow like the wind.

My god! You should have *seen* this poem. How it danced! Synchronized swimming oranges. Finger painting!

And, once it realized—I *would* capture it .... And, for *you!*—What a bucking bronco, throwing its cowpoke! A breaching whale! A ferret, fighting to the death! Ooo!

Nyaah. It didn't stand a chance. But, it didn't give up without a fight.

"Mrow! ...."

"Trreett!?"

"Mrrreow, meooorw ... Rrorww! ..."

"Twrreeter! ... Tree-rr-eee? ..."

Pffftt!!! Its neck——snap.

I present you with this dead poem.

To assure you of my love, I didn't even nibble it, not once!—well, just a little.

I know what you like. A live goldfinch. To stalk; swipe mid-air; to badminton, back and forth between your paws!

But, you weren't there ....

When this Marmalade Toaster Strudel popped up in front of me, we two should have been hiding together in the brush, watching wings gliding, diving ... listening to its warble-trill "... twee treeet ..." Until the pounce! Yesss!

I love how your eyes light up when you see a dead bird. You remember how much fun they are, when they're alive. Pretty, too. Milkweed seeds, drenched in sunset, flying ....

You cry, "Ai! Its life!" when it's gone, when there's no more song. Water creeps in on you, into your crinkles ... fills the corners of your eyes ....

86

March 11, 2020

Wash your hands.

Practice social distancing.

Don't travel unless necessary.

Inform yourself.

Inform others.

Make it your own responsibility to not spread COVID-19.

It's everyone's job to keep people safe in a world pandemic.

The word is out for people to stop meeting in large groups.

My husband keeps going to the Y because the door is open.

An email insisting "we clean all surfaces" is *not* a solution.

The YMCA asks members to "cough correctly"?

The Y should close.

Now.

Measure

I measure my life in unexpected joys.
A letter from my aunt.
The books I open.
Leftover stew.
The last banana, now perfectly ripe.

I measure my days in grandson visits.
Baby smiles,
Baby laughs,
Baby coos.

I only count happiness.
I've learn to fall asleep at the hint of rain.

I run fast to the dead end, because I can.
I'm seeing more lady bugs this year.
I keep up.

We've still got the poor and violence.
We've gone way past the moon and charmed quarks.

Salt burns my eyes every morning.
The bumps on my arm won't go away.

I can't keep up.
Yet, I trust the road will be paved on the car ride home.

I don't add up the endless torments.
My days are few.

I focus on the clear spots in the sky.
I'm out of time to count clouds.

I ignore these crumbs you've left here on the table.
What counts is, you were here with me when they fell.

Meat Alternative

The label says "Live Alfalfa Sprouts," so I listen for the tiny screams as I munch.

Who is to say, the life of an alfalfa sprout is not more worthy than mine? It was raised on a hydroponic farm especially to feed me, and organically, too. For my meal, did I consider alternatives to vegetables, like shrimp, calf, and roe?

What gentle creature has the alfalfa sprout tormented, that I should choose to eat him and spare the others? Has the alfalfa sprout urged his maker to forgive its egregious sins? Has it considered the relative merits of the lives of other creatures and consciously chosen to kill in order to survive, but decided to spare those closest in composition to itself, disregarding, as not requiring careful thought, the lives of those dissimilar to its own reflection in the mirror?

Advertisers tell me, I am one who'd pay a premium for the opportunity to consider myself humane, that I'd want to spare the lives of cows and spined alternatives to sprouts, but I do not buy it.

Advertisers of vegan goods relate heart-rending tales, highlight a woeful "Moo!" or spotlight a suffering goose, forced to feed. They describe a future inspired by love of "all" creatures, insist we produce a kinder, greener planet of healthy plants, not animals, to eat.

Theirs is a lie of greed. Their kind of green grows in banks, and not on the banks that lie sweetly beside flowing, natural waters teeming with lives.

Does the alfalfa sprout not feel the grinding of my molars, scream for mercy at the rending of its body, pray to God for deliverance, and hope, even for resurrection, until the end?

I pray for the alfalfa sprout I devour.

I recall, indigenous people prayed to Mother Earth for food. They apologized to those whose lives they ended. They took only what they needed, ate only so that people could survive.

Missing Her Presence

When my daughter's plane leaves in three weeks,
I'll miss her ineffable presence.

Silence is sure to be roiled in her wake.

Birds outside my window promise,
they'll prompt this silence to deliquesce.
But which bird's song could compare
with her early morning chirrup?

I won't miss, finding in the shower drain,
long, tangled strands of auburn hair, tinged pink,
nor, in the bathroom sink,
foamy gobs of toothpaste and spit.

I'll relish echoes of her naïve, cheery confidence,
that a happy sink-rinser can be counted on to show up,
to faithfully follow in her tousled path,
to wipe up whatever must be wiped up,
if it must be wiped up.

I can't begin to fathom what I'll miss most.

As my daughter leaves home to take on a new job,
a faraway adventure,
despite her mother's impassioned entreaties,
that life would also unfold, closer to home,

what is already gone—and I'm happy to see it leave—
is the fear of a mother
that her daughter might not follow her own dreams.

"Mom, Keep Up the Fight!"

Every time he left for kindergarten, they had bumped fists and shared their chant, "Keep up the fight!" Every time he got home from high school, she had to repeat herself.

"Don't believe that gang!"

"Civilization did NOT end yesterday."

"Don't tell me you will be '... dying any day now!'"

"And, certainly not, '... tomorrow, at the latest!'"

"Good people DO care about you kids."

"We will stop that gang. We will keep up the fight!"

She had to tell the world.

"His last words," said his mother, on TV, "'Mom, keep up the fight!'"

Her eloquent words against gang violence might as well have been a banana—soft and easy to swallow, but not able to pump life's blood through a dead child.

My Husband Loves Me, But He Doesn't Listen

I was mad at him, because he never listens.
His co-workers told him to go to a real flower store.

"My wife is mad at me. I don't know why."
"Two dozen of your wife's favorite flowers will be just perfect.
Does she like roses?"
"Roses? I don't know .... It doesn't matter .... Okay, roses."
"Does she like yellow?"
"Yellow? I don't know .... It doesn't matter .... Okay, yellow."

He handed me the long, white box. *"I bought you roses."*

I'd gushed, that he'd remembered my favorite color, yellow.
Yellow reminds me of the daisies in my wedding bouquet.
The centers of daisies are yellow.

"But, please, no more cut flowers!
I don't want living creatures to die because of me.
And, remember? Save money. We just bought a house.
When we move in, we'll have plenty of free flowers.
The garden is full of my favorites, Black-Eyed Susans!"

When we moved into our new house,
he ripped out the Black-Eyed Susans
and filled the yard with rosebushes.
Red, white, and pink. None were yellow.

"Roses! Your favorite flower! I remembered!"

I smiled and said nothing.
We're still married. Thirty-nine years. But, who's counting?

> *Once I start talking,*
> *he can't understand a word*
> *—my smile enchants him.*

92

My Klein: A Blue Painting Retells an Old Story

The purest blue: Odysseus's wife's untainted nightgown.

The stars map her husband's errant, valiant, homeward crawl.
At each succeeding darkness, his wearied head rests
on a new rock.

Each midnight, as she sits in the sun's quieted chariot,
she channels her curves, aligns them with the galaxies
and hopes he will look up and see and allow the heavens
to lead him home.

Each dawn, her desire lingers in the seat of the chariot,
infused with womanly aroma from the folds of her toga.

The sun searches until it finds Odysseus, cold with longing.
He revives, his heart warmed with lust for her smell.

Recalling the patient motions of her deftly weaving fingers
and the softness of her touch, his sinew swells.

He drags his bones and faithfully follows the sun,
even as it turns slowly, imperceptibly,
every minute of the day leading him off-course.

He's aimed towards a fragrant chariot, where he senses
his wife's faint presence. He's blindly following scents
of home.

Naming the Beasts Post-Fall

Eden's forests rang with beautiful new names.

Jay!
Lark!
Wren!
Nightingale!

Such names touch the tongue lightly. But, at man's fall,
Adam's flight from Eden preceded the release of a truly
terrible, horrible horde.

I've met those awful beasts. They breathe heavily,
lick the sweetness from life, and demand to be named.
My tongue tries taming the untenable, innumerable monsters.

Dad's Alzheimer's
Suprapubic catheter
Hodgkin's lymphoma

Ho! A new arch-demon dog-bull is stampeding through,
trampling, smashing, squeezing out the rest of the strutting,
bold trolls currently tripping, ripping up my tongue.
This name renders.

Bolt Lightning Thor Thundering!
Forest Fires Underbrush Burning!
Shotgun Bambi's Mother Murdering!
Supernova Explosions Everything Destroying!

The tongue revolts, the ear flees. This name flows, pulsing,
lava-burning-acrid-stabbing-its-way-towards-Armageddon-
adrift-in-an-antarctic-sea . . . it is only faintly whispered . . .

h o s   p   i   c   e

n o t
y e   t

I'm not a poet yet
but hope is fading fast

that sanity will hold   out

that   reason ing   will   last

last   lastla
last   last   lala   la

a
la
la
la
la

la   a   ha
st
a la
st a   a

lal a
tt ss
ast   t
la   la   la   t   st la
s   a   t
st

Note to Self

Dear Author of This Volume of Navel-Gazing Poetry,

I wrote these poems when The-Need-To-Process-The-Inexplicable was holding your head underwater.

You're still breathing. You're welcome.

But please don't feel you need to be too critical of the quality of this "poetry." You're still writing. You have plenty of time to redeem yourself as a poet. The other writers in your poetry workshops say you have potential.

Or, you could try going back to computer programming. You did say that was fun. And it will be exciting, discovering all the things they've done with computers since COBOL.

And, you've always said you wanted to get back to painting. You were pretty good in college. You could take another class. Now that you are a senior citizen, tuition at the county college is free. This semester, they are offering a course in watercolors. It's not as hard as it sounds. Using a paintbrush might alleviate some of that inflammation in your hands from spending all day on your iPhone, trying to find something to occupy your time that might hold your interest. You could get fresh air and good exercise walking from the parking lot up the hill to class. And see people.

Or, you could always just go down to the basement, dig up your stash of acrylics and blank canvas, and just start painting again. Buy some new paintbrushes first, I'll bet the old ones are stiff. And, don't worry, you'll get better with practice. And you can enter your work in the county fair under the "Amateur" category. You'd be in great company. All your favorite artists once started out as amateurs.

At least, make a green salad once in a while. You don't even have to leave home to get ingredients. They have veggies available in boxes that come right to your house, pre-chopped, complete with nutritious, delicious recipes.

Just get started and do something. Life is short.

All my love,

    Me

Noter Dame

All my life, I've loved it, since I read a picture book about it. Special windows, sweeping arches, mysterious religious relics, "NOTER DAME."

In grammar school, I wrote about the art and how I loved it, though I'd only seen a picture book about it.

When I learned I hadn't spelt it right—I'd put the "e" before the "r,"—I felt a deep and keen-edged shame. I should have written "Notre Dame" instead of "NOTER DAME."

In college, talking with my friends about our favorite places: rose windows, on my bucket list. I've never had the money, though I wanted, never got to go to visit "NOTER DAME."

I felt a deep and keen-edged shame when I learned I hadn't said it right. I should have called it "Notre Dame" instead of "NOTER DAME."

I'd always hoped to go to France and follow other tourists just to hear the docent say it right, with an accent true François, "Notre Dame."

I learned that we must save the planet and that airplane rides might kill it. And so, I must resist it, never go to visit, see it, "NOTER DAME."

And, now, you're burning!

Damn. I'll never get to go there, see it. I saw the spire, falling through the flame.

All my life, I've loved it, since I read a picture book about it. Special windows. Sweeping arches. Mysterious religious relics. "NOTER DAME."

Obituary

Susanna Lee passed after a career dedicated to intensive research to prepare this obituary. The details do not much matter. They would bore you. Do not give them another thought—life is short.

Your own life is so much more interesting, exciting, salient, complex, relevant, and compelling. Your own joys and pains eclipse anything you could experience vicariously through reading.

Recently, Susanna was just beginning to get to the fun part, having mastered the preliminaries. It was the staying alive part that plagued her at the very end. But, take to heart her observations on the substance of a happy life:

- Nurse your own infants for three years. Then, assume they are changelings. Never forget or let down your guard.

- Your mother was always wrong, because she was always exactly right during her own segment in time and space, which never applied to you or coincided with your situation.

- You, yourself, are the only part of the time/space continuum of which you can be fully aware. You must cope with whatever you find tangential to your own existence.

Feel free to borrow Susanna's To-Do List:

- Love everyone and everything
- Eat only nutritious food
- Dance. Sing. Orgasm. Sleep deep
- Run like the wind at every chance

Omit

All good poems must omit adjectives,
adverbs,
the useless,
the non-descript,
complaints,
varnished memoir,
paper dragons,
tattered overcoats,
weightlessness,
rules,
glass eyes,
stray bullets,
and good cheer.

Except, no. They should include the concrete, including
delimiting tools.

So, tattered overcoats, glass eyes, and stray bullets may stay.

On Fire

His mental illness would not shut up, stand down, and
cooperate, no matter how the yearning for fresh air strangled
him, cut his breath.

I drove home alone after hugging
the released murderer /
husband-killer /
son-stealer /
uncontrollable-temper-in-a-cloud
man.

I hugged him because I could, freely, give him the little I had—
an emptiness in my arm-circle—and the man curled inside, like
the mama cat that crawled inside the bottom lining of the box
spring of my sister's bed, driven by the natural desire to be able
to give birth in isolation.

What better place to bring into the world new life
than suspended on a soft, accommodating, loosely-hung,
absorbent cloth, hanging like a hammock?

The access hole under the bed had been ripped open by the
easy, persistent scratching of bared, naturally sharp claws.

As we released the hug, I saw the sky fill with pink,
omen of God's presence, assurance we are not alone.

We are not solitary, not forgotten, but loved.
Unconditionally, loved.

On Narrowly Escaping Death

It looked so tempting, yet I already knew
how the wind feels, flowing through blonde tresses.

It looked so inviting, yet I'd seen fire escapes,
windows, brick walls, and pavement before.

It looked so refreshing, yet summer was coming,
and I needed sun.

I missed the relief of the drowning roar
of Belmar's breakers.

I missed my mother.
Would she miss me?

Has she felt rain on her own face
on a windy day?

Would she know how far I flew
before I'd broken up and plummeted to earth?

I could hear her,
telling her side to this story,

"Rain doesn't harden into hail by itself,
not without wind to force it up."

On the Way Home From Newark at Dusk

Ebon imprints
are trees,
interruptions
in golden ratio.

The increasingly
pinking horizon
beyond the fields
is too far away
to touch anything
but the heart.

Between the trees
and the train window,
the world
slides by
unnoticed,
unpinked,
and definitely
not glowing.

I look down
and do notice—
there is an emptiness
alongside the tracks.

On Zoom, You Still Don't Take a Bubblebath

As the real slips away
and you want to share more of yourself,
just to feel something,

as your sensual memory starts to fade,
seriously fade,
and you are afraid of losing every caress you ever felt,

every touch,

every slap,

every pointy stick poked in your direction,

every mother's finger wiping up the line of drool sliding down
from the corner of your lip,

you realize,
it's not Zoom.

Your mother's been dead.
Been dead.

It's been a long time since you drooled,
since she saw you drool,
since she noticed you drooling,
since she noticed you.

One Odd Mark

One odd mark, probably deadly melanoma.

I ripped it off my arm; and another one, off my nose.
Too late for testing, it's all gone.

Probably cancerous.
Already spread to my brain, lymph nodes, pancreas.

The stress of worrying about it will probably lead me
straight to immune system failure.

Death soon, no doubt.
Hopefully, before too much pain and suffering.

But, the world will carry on.
I meant to fix it first.

The world, that is.
I meant to fix the world before I die.

Hope I'm wrong about the melanoma.
I couldn't have fixed it anyway.

The world, that is, not the melanoma.
I couldn't have fixed the world anyway.

When people like me would rather
rip off a potentially deadly mole and be rid of it,

neglect to test it to see if it might have killed them,
so they still could treat it, cure it before it's too late,

humans are hopeless.
There's no fixing stupid and anxious and impatient.

No fixing any of it. Nope.

One of Those Stones

As I was walking home on the road, I saw one of those stones. One of those stones that catches your eye and makes you sigh.

"Hi!" I cried, "Ai! One of those stones!"

Oh! If I were three feet high, I'd bend, I'd pick it up. It's one of those stones!

But, now, I'm grown. Now and again, ahead on the road, I'll still see one of those stones. If I'm alone, I'll pause, and gaze—then, stroll on home. Mostly, I leave them alone.

I let them be, where they are. I pass them by. I might kick them, on the sly, with a jealous eye. And, yet, still . . . yes, I still do, I pass them by. I don't stoop, or scoop them up. I leave them be.

Ho! Today! "Here?!" I cry, a hint of a tear in my eye. Here . . . . . . I spy. It's. . . it's . . . one of those stones! My. Oh, my!

I pause. I gaze. To my surprise, I find I'm fine. I do not cry. I let it be and walk on by. But, I do catch my breath.

I pause. Should I turn? Should I return to the spot where I spotted it? Must I leave it? Can't I try to retrieve it? It's one of those stones!

No, I sigh. I won't even try. I leave it.

But . . . Ah. Aah . . . ai!

Imagine . . . I've lived, to see it. I have lived.

To have seen . . . to see . . . to hope. To see again? I might see again—one of those stones!

Pancakes

Mmm, pancakes! Mom's secret was to use a well-seasoned cast iron frying pan, which she primed for the pancake with bacon grease. She smeared it over the entire surface of the pan and heated it to just the right temperature before ladling on a spoonful of batter, just enough to make one medium-sized pancake. She first checked to see if the pan was hot enough, by dipping her fingers into a small bowl of water and flicking a little spritz onto the center of the cast iron. If it sizzled only a little, it was not ready. If it spit and jumped off the pan and right back at her, it was too hot. She'd adjust the heat until it was just right, perfect for browning Side 1 of the pancake and allowing the inside to cook enough to be mostly set. When it was ready, she'd flip it over and brown Side 2. Before turning, she'd check to make sure there were plenty of little bubbles on the surface. This would assure that the inside of the pancake would end up thoroughly cooked, but not before both sides were perfectly browned. She lifted one corner to peek at the underside to make sure. The idea was to never pick up the pancake before the browning was correct, because you couldn't just lay it back down to cook some more. Picking it up too soon or too late, you would lose the sweet, toasted flavor and crispy-edged, chewy texture that makes a pancake perfect.

Pandemic in Perpetuity

My ancestors spent the winter
trying to figure out how
not to freeze to death

while trying to figure out how
not to starve to death.

I've been up since 4:00 a.m.
trying to figure out how
not to eat everything in the house

while trying to figure out how
—while drowning in ennui and anomie—
to occupy my time
in isolation
with nothing to do

and trying to figure out how
to stay awake until 9:00 p.m.
so I can go to bed
and try to stay asleep until 4:00 a.m.
so I can get up

and how
to go back to sleep
because it's not yet 4:00 a.m.
and my mind is open
and I'm in the dark

trying to figure out how
not to bother other humans.

Pandemic Rim Shot

dryer lint	pantyhose
plastic grocery bags	seesaws
Hawaii	tug of war
sheet music	ringside seats
leftover meatloaf	leftover meatloaf
seesaws	boutonnieres
wet umbrellas	sheet music
America's Next Top Model	the High Line
chicken lo mein	cocktail umbrellas

Party Poopers

I threw a summer party, an open house, but the guests,
heedless of my family's traditions, ignored my desires.

I like to keep unbroken, the expanse of my skin.
I prefer it in pristine and smooth "protecting me" condition.

My flesh was pierced by tiny, pointy, swordy things,
then anesthetized with injected buggy spit.

Mosquitoes gorged, as sucking straws,
vacuuming blood through leaky slits.

Lusty feasting rewarded these beastly bugs with satiation.
But, no more!

Not from any stingy, creepy, bitey critters
nor slimy, crawly mites nor winged munchers

will I be accepting
a return brunch invitation.

Pebble

That summer day,
I hung upside-down from the limb over the pond
in Heater's field.

I threw in the last pebble
of the handful I had swiped from your top dresser drawer.

I needed to see,
not the splash,
but concentric circles.

I needed to feel the pale of predictable.
I had to find the steel of even.
I all but imploded, desiring an anti-chaos.

The pebble dropped slowly, unwillingly,
from my open palm.
It sat on the surface of the water for a full two seconds,
then slipped through and disappeared below.

It came right back up,
leapt a foot into the air,
and stopped,
hovering above,
within the arc of the pond's breath.

The pebble was dry.

I could hear its soft rasping,
like the shifting whisper of a damselfly,
asking forgiveness for breaking the tension,
for riling the stillness of the waters.

Peeing in the Street

Despite the fact that all five of them,
both the boys and the girls,

peed in the street
between parked cars,

they led me into a store
and begged the owner

to let the girl from New Jersey
use the bathroom.

Because she's not from here.
And, it's just her.

Not us,
don't worry.

He said, okay.
But, just her.

The anthropologist noted,
the perks of being an alien

include flush toilets, soap and water,
consideration, and privacy.

Perfect Tenderness

O, asparagus, queen of the Kingdom of Nutrition,
I prefer you above all.
You rule over veggies and meat.
The finest delectable treat.

Your perfect tenderness is achieved
by my bending you past your breaking point.
As each matched insect knows its orchid and finds its path in
to where it is sweet,
so I find, by instinct, the location,
the point at which the pressure of my grip
breaks you perfectly into two:
one part delicious, the rest intolerably tough.

Your tasty portion,
I preserve for the bite.

The firm, most rigid remainder, your fibrous stalk
is not nibbled, not even tried, not by the poorest thief.
When my trashcan is scavenged and emptied,
your snapped off bits are all I find on the ground.
Ignored by bears, disdained by rats and raccoons,
forsworn by ravenous crows,
your ends are impossible to eat.

Photo Tips

Look closely. Great photos capture arrangements of light. Look for areas in the scene where there is great contrast. Differently lit leaves, right next to each other. A brightly lit fruit, hanging from a branch in shade. Look for natural lines and interesting shapes. A roof, separating a building from its sky.

Capture whole forms. A whole blossom. A whole door on the front of a skyscraper. A whole boat, floating. Put imagined empty space around the object to frame it.

Look for connections between objects. A stem—what holds it to its leaf? Each, the stem and the leaf, is a separate object. Together, they tell a single story.

Look intensely at whatever is right in front of you. Get curious, even nosy, and ask questions of the scene. Make your photo provide the answer. A puddle—where is the cloud it reflects? The dead fly floating in it—where did it fly when it was alive?

Keep the object as the center of your attention until you learn enough about it to care what happens to it, until you want to share its story with others who are anxious to hear the telling of a good story. Your photo will be only one part of this object's biography. The rest will be filled in by the viewer's history, imagination, and curiosity. Your photo triggers heightened alertness.

Pick the one object in the frame easiest to bring into focus. Make your story about it. As you take its portrait—that object which you see clearly in the light—try to discover its secrets, hidden in the shadows.

Picking at Scabs

A poet asks me, "Can I see your scab? Can I touch it? Can you tell me how it happened? Why don't you leave it alone, instead of picking at it, and just let it heal?"

They actually ask me, "What do you do? Where are you from? Tell me a little about yourself. Why are you here? Why do you enjoy poetry?"

Why can I not answer them simply, "I've lived"?

Instead, I say, "Look." Then, I sharpen my fingernails. I pick up a clean, white canvas and hang it up on the blank wall, opposite the baby grand. I rip off my clothes, scratch open my own chest, pluck out my still beating heart, and hurl it violently across the living room, aiming for the center of the post-modern-art-to-be.

"Are you happy, now?" I ask them.

Oh, they are happy. So happy, they recorded this poem on YouTube.

When I am gone, please send the link to my mother.

Planning for the Tabula Rasa of My Impending Orphandom

I've rescheduled my breakdown
for after my mother's passing
and to coincide with my husband's leaving me.

The sound of the whetting of kitchen knives
could mean sliced steak for lunch
or a long overdue throat slitting.

I'm planning ahead,
but I don't promise
to be available past four.

The waves of the ocean call.
Dare I tiptoe in?
Close enough to feel the breakers?

"Irresistible" used to refer to pleasures.
It wasn't a measurement of the sureness
of death.

Poem for the Ignoble Flu

I don't have an avatar.
I don't have a lover.
I don't have a dollar.

I don't dabble in plastic.
I don't paint my nails.
I don't wear fake bunny ears to my selfies.

Since I read all those classics, did my mind turn to stone?
If I stay by myself, won't I be alone?

I won't eat excuses.
I won't carry stars.
I finally decided who I am. Who you are.

I'm here on this planet, as far as I know.

It won't make a difference if I carry this thought
out into a poem.

Poetry Police

When you're reading poetry, especially one of my books, you'll run into a poem every once in a while that just doesn't make sense, no matter how many times you read it.

So, I'll apologize now.

I'm so sorry if I lost you with that last poem of mine.
Feel free to select as many as you'd like
from my list of standardized excuses:

- I meant to send that poem to *The New Yorker*

- I'm writing about something I really don't care to share

- I wrote that poem to confuse you

- You missed a cultural reference. You need to get out more

- That poem was supposed to be funny

- You missed a literary reference. This surprises me

- You've discovered a gap in my knowledge base. There are many

- You've caught me in a lie, oops!

- I have my own unique definitions for words

- In indulging in abstruse literary devices, I've confused you

- I'm playing with words—their sounds or their meanings (or both! lol)

- I've mislaid a comma (my personal favorite!)

Don't be alarmed. The Poetry Police will be here momentarily to sort it all out.

Nothing to see here. Move along, move along.

Privilege

This poem reeks of privilege.
Can you smell it?

The fresh-brewed coffee
held in a pure white mug
warming my soft hands.

I write my poetry on the same smartphone
I use to summon books,
fresh cut flowers,
vacations to sandy beaches,
fond memories,
and the poetry of other poets.

This screen can also shriek with news of the horrid,
terrible things
that are happening everywhere else
but not right here.

And, whenever I've had enough
of reading about other people,
I can pull back
and write whatever I want,
whatever I want to see,
see right here,
here on my screen.

I'm planning to spend this winter perfecting this poem.

This poem absolutely reeks of privilege.
I can't stand it.

Protest

Naked, she is not giggling girlishly.
She's poised, comfortable in her own skin.

She did not choose "Dare," playing Truth-or-Dare.
She is not incompetent at poker, playing Strip Poker.
This is not a game.

Ah . . . She's a priest.

Though, that can't be right!
She's a woman. She's not allowed to be a priest.

But, she's a rebel.

Yes, she's a priest. She has decided for herself.
She has taken a vow to wear the cloth.

Until that's allowed,
she will wear nothing.

QUEEN OF CORONA

I spend pandemic evenings alone, here in my library,
spread out in my favorite chair, watching TV,
eating corn chips, cheddar, and salsa,
a twist of lime in my Corona,
watching Fred Astaire
on Amazon Prime
and Jeopardy
and news,
reading
poetry,
Twitter,
Facebook,
old classics,
and magazines,
Zooming with poets
and the extended family,
shopping online and on apps
for fresh veggies and toilet paper,
staring at clothes I don't get to try on,
salivating over books to read if I don't die,
and deciding on which pre-existing condition to
cultivate next. What would make me most likely to die
of corona quickly, shorten my merry-go-round ride in hell?

Rainbow

When you're looking for a rainbow,
for confirmation your prayers have been answered,
open your eyes and look up,

away from the earth,
beyond every misbegotten thing on it,
past darkened, sifted clouds,

and stare at the nothing place.
You might find remnants of once threatening rain.
See? It did not have the heart to fall on you.

Turn your face away from where you'd expect to see
an illuminating sun.
Search the wide air, the space above the settled horizon.

Search the void of everything.
Here, in this empty spot, will be the evidence,
if your promised miracle is indeed manifest.

Normally, you won't find anything there,
anything at all,
much less, anything extraordinary.

Recipe

Begin empty.

Add silence.

Slice truth into atomic cycles.

Inoculate the ardent against escape.

Separate each valley from its promises.

Add stars à le monde to the sordid.

Placate the losing tortoise/hare bettors.

Stir-fry the double-parked.

Marinate the chosen few. First, tie them up with lace curtains.

Scrape a red beet into a watched pot.

Add pi tears of joy.

Sift moon rocks until doubled.

Lunge into the next understatement.

Set the timer for blue.

Salute the ears lining the walls.

Garnish with striped bendy straws.

Serves: Seven birds or one romantic.

Call it off.

Say "Uncle!"

Moms and dads, teach your boys and girls, both, fighting rules.
To listen for "Uncle!" and say it when you lose.

When the "Uncle!" is said, the fighting is over.
Get up and let your opponent recover.

Boys, you know when the fighting is done.
After the "Uncle!" more fighting's not fun.

Girls, learn to fight fair, follow rules like the boys.
Say "Uncle!" Then, stop and go play with your toys.

When you hear "Uncle!" cried, one's admitted they've lost.
Show respect for the loser, don't increase the cost.

Know when it's time to quit, time to just go.
Don't permanently harm a temporary foe.

It's called fighting fair, leave the loser alone.
Let girls in on the game—let them fight—then go home.

Seeing My Own Blood Outside My Body

All that has happened to me is unique and unrequited,
and no one has heard me.

But, you, Dear Reader, you are my captive, my listener.

I have seen a chaos of stars in a moonless, cloudless sky;
the white tail of a doe, bounding in fear;
a cat, carrying in her mouth a kitten she has limped;
and a child, splashing in a puddle, where that child was me.

I have seen blood escaping from a body that was not mine;
and blood—that used to be hidden under my own skin—
outside, unprotected.

I have dreamed the world was melting. I saw the horizon red—
streams of lava spouted skyward, as on a Jupiter moon; Earth's
crust, falling away, the crumbling edge rushing toward me . . .
and my mother, holding my hand, urging me to run with her
in the direction of hope, where we'd stand a chance of taking
the most breaths before our last . . .

. . . awestruck extra-terrestrials hovered above us, up in their
spaceship, observing us closely, glad to be capturing the human
miracle. They sent me their message of rescue telepathically.

Keep going, we'll pick you up.

I draw you this picture with words, knowing words fail.

I write anyway.

On seeing my own blood outside my body, I gagged a little.
I've kept my eyes open ever since, in awe of the unknown,
of what's to come, not wanting to miss a thing.

Self-Deprecation

A woman says she's blind to the charms of womankind
and denies her "normal" body has appeal.

She'll decry, as just a myth, there are magnets in her kiss,
and she cannot comprehend her lover's zeal.

There is no hypnotic vise to be discovered in her eyes,
nor glue to hold him plastered to her lips.

She'll disown her mighty power to make her lover cower
by threatening to deny him breasts or hips.

She must use her feminine wile to subdue the ardent male,
who, all day and night, is proving he's a pest.

He is tethered to her thighs, reveling in her exhaled sighs,
and she never, never ever, gets to rest.

Seppuku Poem

That last line of your poem,
like a seppuku sword,

stabbed me; it ran me through,
my own hand on the hilt.

The blade tore a slice in my skin
as it pulled from one side of my gut to the other.

Then it ripped straight up to my chest,
revealing my heart.

I lay, opened,
listening to your poem.

The blade turned and ran backward
along the same path, back down toward my gut.

My other hand followed the blade,
sewing my skin closed.

The tip of the sword worked its way out
slowly, steadily.

By the time the tip was freed,
I'd completely sewn shut the hole.

The sword left no scar, no mark.
There wasn't even any muss to clean up.

The echo of your poem remains inside,
my heart captive.

Your last line is still slicing,
a torturous thousand internal cuts.

Seven True Stories of Eve and Mary

I.   In Eden, Eve plays with a kitten. She strokes her pussy and experiences pure joy.

II.   Time passes. The kitten grows into a cat. It hisses. "God! WTF! Is your 'Time' thingie going to do this to every pussy?" Her eyes opened, Eve bails from The Garden.

III.   God quizzes Adam over Eve's disappearance. "I haven't seen Eve in a long time. Where in Hell is she?" Adam retells Eve's story, but relates his own version, "Eve's Evil Pussy."

IV.   Time passes. They find Eve. Her version of the story differs considerably from Adam's. No one believes her tale, "The Evils of Time."

V.   Time passes. By now, everyone has heard Adam recite his poem, "Eve's Evil Pussy."

VI.   Time passes. Called "Adam's Law," any woman who lets anyone except her husband stroke her pussy is stoned to death.

VII.   Time passes. Mary is unwed and pregnant. Facing death by stoning, she writes a poem, "Virgin Pussy Birth." Awed, God publishes it in his next anthology.

Sister Survivors

Unseen denizens of my neighborhood thrive, hidden in
yellowed January lawns. Worms, bugs, beetles, and spiders
feast on frigid detritus and grow into morsels fit for a bird.

The fattest crow I've seen so far this year struts in a random
stride, this way and that, below my picture window, jabbing
at the ground. It scoops up companions for breakfast.

It holds each for a moment, between maxilla and mandible—the
two pointed halves of its beak. It regards, for an instant, whether
its mouth holds an edible, then throws back its head and parts
its bill a bit wider.

The bird and the bug, mismatched creatures, have little time for
conversation, the smaller is so quickly slipped inside, between
the two horned tongs, and advanced into the craw.

The crow allows gravity to do the dirty work of prodding the
critter into descending the gullet. A snap of the beak finalizes
the arrangement.

A second crow—its zig-zag path also unpredictable—meanders,
covering the same ground in a different pattern, scooping up
sister survivors of the still-prancing, shiny-feathered, first
fat diner.

SNAFU

Sitting on a hilltop,
waiting for the end of the world,
a familiar occupation throughout time.

For thousands of years, people like me
have been sitting on hilltops, alone or in crowds,
waiting for the end of the world,

while the rest of the people keep going to work,
continue eating and drinking,
and never stop making love.

If they'd notice people like me, they'd hesitate,
pause in their work, swallow the bite they were chewing,
not take another sip of their wine nor kiss their dear once more,

and remark to themselves and their peers,
"Isn't it crazy how there are people sitting on hilltops
waiting for the end of the world?"

fully confident they could keep on working and eating
and drinking and making love and freely kissing their dears,
as, clearly, the world had never ended before.

Spring Show

The clocks are crazy. The sun leaps out of bed.
The sky picks up a southern accent.
A bit brighter than yesterday, a truer blue.

A late-March morning hangs mid-air,
swirling pink and wispy clouds, sweeping the ground.
Fred Astaire's partner swishes circles of chiffon.

Tiny buds puff themselves up
to make their debut on the spring carpet.
Like synchronized swimmers, petals part.

Blossoms exude perfume.
Abuzz with excitement, insect escorts hover.
Flowers believe their promises of fruits.

The live audience grows wild.
Dandelions and daffodils dance in the aisles,
their gold chapeaus now part of the show.

Bushes and trees unfurl leaves the lightest of greens.
Oscar de la Renta and Pantone take notes on hues.
Politicians take notes on seduction.

Robins showed up first, to rave reviews.
Their breasts blush.
Their breath smells of worms.

Summer Evening Storm

After fixing broken software all day on Wall Street,
then waiting for my bus—it never came—
I squeezed onto a subway of commuters.
Summer thunder clapped, then followed up with rain.

At Penn Station, I found a bus. Got back to Jersey.
Flung my sweaty self into my car's front bucket seat.
But before I'd climbed the two flights to our condo,
a cloudburst drenched my briefcase. Oh, great. Defeat.

You met me at the door: A kiss. A smile.
Took off my foggy glasses, wet stockings, and soggy dress.
Poured the wine. Served me spaghetti and a salad.
Then gave me what I wanted—your caress.

When lightning quit its striking,
we two lit up cigarettes.

Summer, Sussex County, New Jersey

Mow the lawn.
Catch fireflies.
Eat s'mores.
Garden.
Swear.
Read.
Nap.
Run.
Race.
Whistle.
Go fishing.
Ride a horse.
Wish on a star.
Ride your bike.
Play freeze tag.
Play four square.
Go to the library.
Tie-dye a t-shirt.
Leap over a log.
Bask in the sun.
Sleep in a tent.
Make a wish.
Catch frogs.
Skip rope.
Swim.
Play.

Raft
down
the
Delaware
River
past
the
Water
Gap.

Swat mosquitos.
Smash a deer with your car.
Pitch horseshoes at the neighbors'.
Swap ghost stories around a campfire.
Watch fireworks. Race your paper boat.
Skip stones on the pond. Watch the ripples.
Swerve the wheel to avoid hitting the turkeys.
Stare at phosphorescent rocks under black light.
Attend a baseball game at Skylands Stadium.
Stretch your arms around the tree's trunk.
Bake a peach pie with a lattice crust.
Blow all the fluff off dandelions.
Act in summer stock theatre.
Sell things at a flea market.
Practice your times tables.
Climb up to the tree fort.
Man a lemonade stand.
Play Hide-and-Seek.
Write in your diary.
Fold an origami swan.
Attend an estate auction.
Hike the Appalachian Trail.
Draw a picture of your family.
Try on diamonds at a jewelry store.
Join a pig roast at an abandoned farm.
Drop stones in the pond. Make a big splash.
Paint a picture on a flat rock with a wet cattail.
Ask your grandmother how to live to be a hundred.
Vote for Queen of the Fair at the Farm and Horse Show.
Hike up to Sunrise Mountain before dawn. Stay past sunset.

Swept Away

Oh, to be swept away
by a stampede!

Like-minded folk
converging
on a particular point on earth
I happen to occupy,
ignoring me, rushing
on their way
away from
what it's imperative
to run away from,

sweeping me off my feet
and dragging me with them
without a destination,
away from danger,
on the path
to escape!

Oh, to be so close
to such surety!

Oh, to realize there is such confidence,
a confidence, in knowing what it is that must be avoided.

Oh, that such a confidence exists!

Tai Chi

I'm standing in the forest
in my tai chi class.

My feet are bent.
I feel my soles squish sands at Belmar Beach.

Each toe digs.
Deep. Deep. Deep.

The tide goes out.
Comes in.

Water,
flowing endlessly.

It's tai chi.
The instructor does not interrupt my reverie.

He doesn't have to speak to remind me of the tide,
the in and the out, the circular motion of the living ocean.

My breath
flows freely,

exhaled out,
drawn inside me,

around and round in effortless waves,
invisible lines of infinity.

Not like in my aerobics class.
There, every time, they chide me,

"Now, don't forget to breathe!
Breathe! Breathe! Breathe! Breathe!"

Testing, Testing

Last year, my mother had a test,
and, although the rest of the results looked fine,
her hemoglobin was a little high; they don't know why.
This year, it's much lower, but still, it's in range.
To her doctor, however, lower looks strange.
He wants to do another test.
Until they find out why her hemoglobin acts so strange,
even if it is in range,
they want to do test after test after test.

I can see why doctors might want to know.
They'd like a chance to cure you, to prove Death hasn't won.
When they don't find, in testing, something to heal,
they like to pursue with more testing, with zeal.

The stress of not testing, of not knowing what to fear,
if there is something in there that might kill you,
something doctors could fight, if only they knew,
that alone might keep you up at night.

"It tests your patience, waiting to see the doctor,
or for the nurse to take your blood.
And, of course, you can't have any food.
And then you have to wait again, for the biopsy to heal.

"Why can't they look at *me*? I'm eighty-four.
When I was eighty-three, my blood was fine!
I'm older, can't that be the reason why?
Everything else is fading. What if hemoglobin, too,
is giving up without a fight, like hearing and eyesight?
And, what if it is, 'internal bleeding?' I can live with that.
But, anesthesia, for endoscopy? Can't that kill me?
And colonoscopy? I'd rather dance with Death
than take another chance with anesthesia!

"I don't want doctors just guessing how much testing I can take
before I don't wake up, from testing, for testing's sake."

The Aside

To be, or not to be unique, that is the question.

Whether 'tis nobler to be one's own true self
or to flounder in a sea of otherness—afloat, adrift,
as one more shipwrecked manifest of loneliness
amidst those who have no idea of what we think,
those who cannot fathom this deep well, from which we drink.

Asleep, they do not see our dreams.

We tread on water they see porous.

Our ears hear different songs, a different chorus.

We find, no soulmate leans in our direction.

We yearn to stir the others' insurrection,
to untie the ropes which bind men's minds
and hold them closed.

We hope unceasingly to make a difference:
to find them wakened to our heart's desire,
their minds afire with love and gentle understanding,
complete acceptance.

The Beautiful Game

I. Practice

Game, I study you in fevered pitch.

Gravity, unseen faithful companion,
you lurk, ever present.

Maths, I long to know you and learn
your calculus.

Game, give up your secrets!

II. Game Time

These blades of grass, united into an army,
fight my cleats!

Everywhere—toes! toes! toes!
Mine, friends', foes' . . .

. . . an opening!
. . . . just one more crack . . .

Dash . . . !. . . . . . . SMASH!!!

III. Reflection Reflection Reflection

"Clock time" is just a suggestion.

For this, I run, swim winter laps, gasp . . .
. . . everything . . . . my soul . . .

The Destroyer

I must have written thousands of poems,
each one exquisite, brimful of meaning,
telling the stories of human existence,
the depth of our feelings, expressing it all.
Each poem finished was honed to perfection,
brilliantly shining, primed with excitement.
Each anxious word sat, quietly waiting,
expecting its entrance, balanced and poised.

Its fellow words, I had lined up quite neatly.
Each one precise, I was sure of its meaning.
Alone, they were nothing. Yet, tied all together,
potions of magic, inspiring, became.
Waiting to come out, enlighten the audience
(the reader, in ignorance, cherishing bliss),
my words were not frightened, my poems, an army,
well-trained, determined; their mission: world peace.

Then, mass devastation! Self-doubt roared in, ruthless,
enveloped my poems, "Select All | Delete,"
controlled my computer, devoured my files,
crept in and erased them. It conned me, this thief.
Thus, came The Destroyer, my syllable nemesis.
No friend of creation, it stole every gem.
It even ate innocent poems, like haiku.
Assumed all were gutless and meaningless tripe.

If, somehow, this poem escaped The Destroyer
and made it to your ears, don't think, "It's all right."
Countless great treasures more beauteous than sunlight,
insightful, wise, thoughtful, were rolled out before.
This one escaped noticed because it was weaker,
no glimmer of genius, no power to behold.
Do not be content with this witless pretender.
Those other, dead, poems were worth so much more.

The Elements of Storytelling

Watching a butterfly
fold and unfold its wings,
poetry taught me this:
It's grand to die of heartache
or to live, trying,
watching a butterfly
fold and unfold its wings.

Watching a butterfly
fold and unfold its wings,
poetry taught me this:
It's grand to die of heartache.

Watching a butterfly
fold and unfold its wings,
over and over,
my father,
ill with Alzheimer's Disease,
tells his stories,
watching a butterfly
fold and unfold its wings.

Watching a butterfly
fold and unfold its wings,
poetry taught me this:

Watching a butterfly
fold and unfold its wings,
poetry taught me this:
It's grand to die of heartache
or to live, trying,
watching a butterfly
fold and unfold its wings.

The Girl Who Stepped Down Off the Bus

The curvy girl in the tight, white t-shirt and gloving blue jeans
steps down off the New York City bus.

I stare, entranced, not twenty feet from this goddess.

She's searching the street as if today is her birthday
and this might be a surprise party.

Is she new in town, deciding who she should make
her very first friend in the city?

"Pick me! Pick me!"

Her eyes hover over the crowd.
She's a summer shower, deciding where to rain.

She weaves through the noontime throng
as if bobbing over the ocean's breakers.

I'm a stranger, adoring her every motion.

She's tossing her head to keep her curls free
from becoming entangled in the straps of her backpack.

A lock of her hair brushes my chin as she glides past.

The Matriarch

No one asks the Matriarch for her résumé,
her references, or a list of her qualifications.

No cover letter could lay out the reasons
she is a good fit for the position.

She completes no job application,
no background check or physical.

No one needs her social media passwords
to see how she interacts with people.

Her strengths are apparent. She is not interviewed.
She has no weaknesses to be discovered.

No one pries, searching for character flaws.
There are no skeletons hidden in her closet.

There is no FBI file with her name on it, to surface.
No one dare ask her to submit ten years of tax returns.

Her kind of cheek cannot be swabbed for DNA.
Blood tests would yield no evidence of self-medication.

The Matriarch faces no competition.
All readily accept, without reservation, the Matriarch.

The Perfect Bowl of Cereal No Longer Exists

The right amount
of Rice Krispies,

lightly sprinkled,
just so,
with sugar

over
just ripe
bananas,
sliced
to just the right thickness,

the milk,
gently splashed
to moisten the sweet bits
and dampen the crunchy bits.

Dig in,
spoonful
by perfectly balanced
spoonful,

with my dad,
who's shown me how
to breakfast
as a god
with gods.

The Recliner

Old and retired and sitting in your recliner
while keeping weeping to a minimum,

you wish your wife would go shopping for the day
in the city with her sister

and not try to show you what she bought
or describe for you

the salesgirl's red crooked lipstick
or the bags under her eyes,

or attempt to mimic
her screechy little laugh

so you could hear it,
as if you were there.

The Sadness of Fast Cats

The cheetah has the most perfectly formed body of all beings.
Expending the fewest calories possible, it springs into action,
defying gravity, using friction to best advantage.

It soars across the veldt, taking for its dinner
whatever its fancy strikes.

No need for always hauling stores of fat to tide it over,
it is lean and carries its full weight effortlessly.

The big cat is always ready to start.
Its trim muscles excite at the whiff of eland.

But, it only starts when reminded of hunger, only when driven.
It's only driven by need to eat, not driven always.

It never runs just for fun, just because it can,
just because it is the fastest thing.

It never strolls without purpose,
just out of curiosity, just to see what's out there.

Its paws never hit the ground running.
They are clearly made for silent stalking.
Cheetahs stalk at the whiff of prey.
They break into a run only for the chase, for the kill.

Cheetah kittens are not yet big cats. They practice at being cats,
stalking, pouncing, prancing, watching, sniffing, listening,
crouching perfectly still, watching, watching,
turning their ears this way and that, twitching their tails.

The big cat sleeps and eats, sleeps and eats, sleeps and eats.

It never runs just for fun, just because it can,
just because it is the fastest thing.

The Spokes on My Bike

The spokes on my bike were bare,

though I could have bejeweled them
to dazzle in the sun

or attached playing cards on clothespins
to make a snapping sound when the wheels spun.

I didn't notice
whether it was clouds or the sun
that had my back.

I rode my bike.

Wild!
Fast!
Free!

I rode my bike like I was never coming back.

The Starter Is Dead

I've let it go too long. The sourdough starter is dead.
In its jar on the shelf, behind eggs and the milk and some jam,
the starter is hidden, and no one would dare throw it out.
But, it doesn't remind me that it needs to breathe.
It needs to be fed, and it needs to be stirred.
So, the sourdough starter is dead,
though I meant to bake bread every day,
every day when I got out of bed.
But, it's been neglected for over two years, and surely it's dead.

And so is my father.
And, almost, my mother.
Both from lymphoma.
And I am so close to forgetting to keep me alive.

The starter is dead.
Been ignored and not fed and never stirred once in two years.
So now, is it dead, just as I'd feared?
I'd kept it alive for almost a year.
I'd baked bread and fed it.
I kept it alive for almost a year.
I might be too hasty, to throw it away.
I could try tomorrow.
Just pry off the lid.
Add some flour and water and stir for a minute.
Then let it sit out for a day.
If the sourdough starter is given a chance—a new stirring
and feeding and time for its rising—the bread could be tasty.
Today, I will plan it.
I'll set out the flour and measure the water.
I'll warm up the starter and see.
If it isn't too late for the starter to rise
and it isn't too late to try just one more time,
then isn't there something else more I could try?
If I were wise, I could try a new rising, try to do something.
What could I do that might open *your* eyes?
It might be surprising to find there's a new you-and-me.

The Tear That Threatens to Not Fall

I suspect this tear that threatens to not fall
is a relic from the past

when I discovered the giggle of lover's voices
behind the attic door.

Or, is it the kitten, remnant of a mother's rejection,
—of the four kittens, none were nursed—
is this the last, the one I tried to nurse, to save,
the one that died, not at its mother's feet,
but at my pre-teen chest?

Or, is this the reflection of the me-child,
leaning over a footbridge, studying a string?
The string is still.
The string is not yet wriggling.

It hangs, as I hold it, with the promise of a fish.

How long was it,
I held onto that string?

How was it, I finally . . .
how could I . . .
when did I . . .

let it go?

Three Forty-Eight

It
is three
forty-eight AM,
and the man I would
like to again call snuggle-bunny
trudges down the hall in flip-flops to pee
in the bathroom on the other side of the kitchen
so he won't wake me up and give me yet one more
reason to complain. He seems to suffer, unbearably, on
hearing the sound of my voice at any time of the day or night.
I gift the old man my silence in the no-silence flop, flop, flop,
flop, flop, flop, flop, flop,
flop, flop, flop, flop, flop, flop, flop, flop, op,
flop, flop, flop, flop, flop, flop, flop, flop
flop, flop, flop, flop, flop, flop, flop,
flop, flop, flop, flop, flop, flop,
flop, flop, flop, flop, flop,
flop, flop, flop, flop,
flop, flop, flop,
flop, flop
flop, f,
lop,
f.

Tiara Sublet

I'd long been denied the truth:
I was born to live in crowds.

I left my tribe behind
and went to seek my glass roots.

I bathed in the Fountain of Youth.
I wore a third-eye tattoo.
I played music—wooden maracas.

Basking in the sun
under my frond-waving Adonis,
I read my signed, first-edition *Just Desserts*.
It was penned by a regular at Turtleback Zoo.

On the last page,
scrawled in blue ink,
my favorite haiku:

> *Bacon.*
> *Perfectly crisped.*
> *Still warm.*

Tilt

The tiny windmill never turns.
There are no winds but poet breath.

Frigid desert nights
cannot quench the fire of trust.

The ass plods on, always hoping,
hoping it's time for oats.

The stars burst open.
Tears of heaven flood the plain.

Dulcinea spreads her apron
and dries it all,

the morning dew,
the evening rain.

Time Has No End

Have you seen the tattoo over my heart?
It does not say "DNR," but "Keep trying!"

Do not be quick to pull the plug.
Turn up the music. I must remember where I am.

Where else would birds fly,
but where it's empty?

Where else would I go,
but to stay forever inside this human body?

Where else, but inside their shells, empty of all but turtle,
would turtles dance?

I am a turtle.
I balance the weight of the universe on the back of my shell.

I set down my shell, but not to rest.
Inside, I dance.

My shell can barely contain my tarantella!
The whole universe sits on me, a turtle dancing.

I dance, and the universe rocks.
On my tattooed shell, it says, "Keep trying!"

To My Childless Child

I have so much to tell your grandchild,
my dear great-grandchild,
who will not breathe their first breath
before I've drawn my last,
of all I know, how I knew everything
before I became a parent
—how I knew nothing.

My child, you, who are convinced, as I was,
that there is no more to know, please
give your grandchild a chance at life.

Offspring of your offspring will know more than I,
more than you could ever imagine now.
They will be beautiful.
They will be full of knowledge.
They and theirs will rewrite history,
find new ways to define "wisdom," "love," and "peace."

They will create new words to inspire desire for creation.

Today I Woke up Twice

At midnight,
a terrifying vision.

I heard my sister's voice,
"Come! Quickly! There's a problem in Room 266!"

I've been visiting Room 266, my father,
all week.

He lingers in a hospital fog
of Too Little Urine Passing with a pinch of Not Moving

and complications
of Alzheimer's Dementia.

He's singed.
Now and then, he suffers a twinge or a pang.

He's been forced to stay, to lay tethered to his hospital bed,
for a week.

A week. That's all it takes
to turn a robust 86-year-old woodchopping man into weak.

Exhausted,
I fell back to sleep.

The terrifying vision on my second awakening
—no less frightening—

the birthing,
the terrible trauma of releasing this newborn poem.

Tossed Salad

At the salad bar,
I look for water droplets on the plates,
freezer-burned edges on the lettuce,
clumped shredded carrots,
wilted greens,
overgrown bean sprouts,
underripe tomatoes,
toddler, not baby, spinach,
smashed green olives,
burnt crust on the mac-n-cheese,
spots cut out from the red beets,
wings and other insect fragments,
still-motile creepy crawlies,
chick peas in the vinaigrette,
too-ambitious roots on the radishes,
surliness in the salad-bar replenisher,
bigger-than-bite-sized croutons,
drips of Creamy Ranch in the Russian,
looks of disgust on the faces of other salad bar patrons,
and other deal-breakers.

Train Wreck

That night,
I saw my face in the mirror
as I realized,
the screeching of the brakes
was nothing but an annoying noise.

I was powerless to stop the train
that would hit your car
and steal your life.

That bathroom mirror
revealed my horror
as I realized,
there was no train,
no car,
no brakes.

The screeching noise
coming from my mouth
was but useless,
as silence.

You were deafened
by a siren call:

heroin,
claiming you back.

Trump

Mom's bridge club is coming.
Nothing trumps that.

Clean!
Everything else can wait.

Leave no evidence eight children live here,
no matter that you have more homework to do.

Outline your English term paper in your head
while you scrape dried milk from a wooden high chair.

Practice your seven times tables aloud
while you press tarnish stains from the good silver.

Decide what you want to be when you grow up
as you scrub fingerprints off light switches.

After you help mom prepare for her bridge club,
you have the rest of your life to prepare for the rest of your life.

While enveloped in senseless, onerous chores, contemplate
how easy it is to avoid senseless, onerous chores.

Just clean up as you go, right after you eat, right after you play,
right after you put the baby in her crib.

Why wouldn't you wipe up spilled milk
before it has a chance to dry?

Trust in the Moon

All my life, I've trusted in the moon.

I stamp my feet in puddles just to see it dance.

I know it's just the moon's reflection.
I trust I cannot break the moon I cannot touch.

I splash.
I break the moon free
from its encircling fence.

Moonlight arcs in streaking ripples;
semicircles skirt away from my feet.

The glowing, above, never moves
from its hovering, watchful place.

It's faithful, never doubting in its mission,
confident it will always sail over me.
I will not slip away beyond its reach.

In the rocking arms of the cloudless sky,
the moon is carried,

growing larger, waning,
disappearing, and returning,

eternally repeating,
in its own moonlike fashion,
what it knows it does right,

without questioning
why others might question
why it does what it does.

Trusting Detritus

My favorite log of all time
has pale green lichen over almost all of it,
but it's basically solid and dry.

I can find it every time I scavenge for firewood
behind our campsite at Stokes State Forest.
It points the way back.

It doesn't teeter when I walk the length of its spine.
It had fallen on level ground.

It has always been a pirate's gangplank for me
whenever I've needed one.

I can trust it
not to fall apart.

Bits of lichen break off under my sneakers,
but they always grow back.

My kids laugh at the ridiculous notion,
a person could get lost in the woods
or would come to love the peculiar way
a piece of detritus gathers meaning over time.

Trusting detritus seems like crazy talk, I guess,
easy advice to discard.

Tumbling

Tumbling head over heels,
I fell in love with the art of karate.

I discovered I could roll.

I learned
to defend myself long enough to buy time,
to know when to run away,
to protect my head at all costs,
to keep the enemy in sight,
and to read my opponent.

Tumbling head over heels
in love with the game of tennis,
I realized, I'd finally learned

my backhand from my forehand,
to lob, to catch my breath,
and to read my opponent.

Then, in a real life tumble, playing tennis,
head over heels across the court, I rolled
and leapt to my feet, unharmed.

I learned,
I was lucky to be able to walk away.

Now, I've mastered the rules of The Game.
I watch for new trickery
from Gravity and Time
as they learn to read me.

It's time to switch from tennis to tai chi.

Vignettes From a Pandemic

Preparing to die alone unprepared to die.

Strangers on YouTube taking their last breaths.

Hugging my kids, possibly to death, sharing a pizza.

My husband mowing the lawn. My husband gardening.

Poetry on Zoom. Not signing up for next semester.

My grandson born without Susanna Nana in attendance.

My husband baking bread and watering the plants.

No grandkids in costume at our door on Halloween.

My husband shopping at Lowes for more houseplants.

The dog's last vet visit. We run out of yeast.

My husband pacing the floor; him, washing the floor.

My husband buying houseplants, pacing the floor.

My husband watering the houseplants, pacing, gardening in the
snow, watering, watering the plants.

My husband pacing the floor. My husband gardening.

My husband mowing the neighbor's lawn.

Not walking my daughter down the aisle.
No Zoom, either. The kids want to be "in the moment."

My husband pacing the floor. My husband pacing.

Self-publishing the thawing manuscripts, my life's work.

Voodoo

I'm holding voodoo in reserve
to vanquish those who **do** deserve the evil touch.

I don't respect those who make each other suffer.
I hang out with those who love. We try to fix human woes.

But, who knows?

If someone tricks me or my brothers, sisters, or others
and I find they've come to harm,
I'll practice voodoo.

I've a charm that's rather dandy,
and these pins will come in handy
if there's someone who needs fixing.

Voodoo's very simple.
You could learn it in one night.

Online, they have instructions,
how to hex folks who vex you.

Don't cross my path the wrong way.
Voodoo's out there.
You **will** pay.

Wake When You Are Ready

In bed,
tai chi.

What a wonderful way
to wake up.

The form is simple.
Movement.

To allow you to wake up
each part of your body

when you are ready.
Feel.

Your whole body is energy.
Breathe.

Move.
Feel your own energy.

Now,
feet on the floor,

one
at a time.

Warm

Two mugs of milk and chocolate.
Marshmallows.

A fire lit.
A pile of logs by the fireplace.

A poker for stirring.
Your glowing face.

Extra-thick sliced homemade bread.
Peanut butter and honey, spread.

My younger self once made this quilt.
Your pjs, plaid; mine, blue silk.

Tomorrow, we'll go out, shovel snow.

This novel, written centuries ago,
I've already read, but trice.

This winter evening . . . feels nice.

Warmth

I close the bathroom window,
switch on the heat lamp on the ceiling,
go out and shut the door
and wait twenty minutes,

so . . .

when I fetch my mother from her bed,
hold her up under her arms,
hold her close, hugging her from behind,
and waddle with her
slowly,
step by step,
out of the bedroom
and down the hall,

and we turn left
and keep going,
keep waddling
until we arrive at the bathroom
and I open the door,

we will waddle in
together,
and I will hear

"Aah,"

"Warm,"

just what she needs
for her sponge bath
on the shower chair.

We Fell Out of the Gondola

Let's just tell the kids you love me, I love you, but we didn't
know until we had that accident skiing in the Alps.

. . . No. Make it . . . scuba diving in the Everglades.

Scratch that. We were in Australia. Or, maybe, Antarctica?

Yes, it was . . . Antarctica. They know Antarctica is on my
bucket list. I hate the cold, but I love clean. They have the
fewest spiders in the world, per square foot, in Antarctica.

Let's just tell the kids we were checking out the vanishing
species in the falling ice shelf, recording them for science —
saving them, we'd hoped, just in case there's still people here to
keep our DNA company, someday, just before it all goes bust.

Let's just tell our friends to tell our kids we found God, hiking
El Camino, and took ourselves and the Good News to the
farthest reaches of Pluto's orbit to smear discovery out there,
to besmirch the galaxy before somebody else does, but we ran
out of fuel, forgetting solar batteries don't charge themselves
without a sun.

Will the kids believe that? Didn't we teach them to believe
nothing at all?

Let's just leave the kids a note—hide it behind a valuable
painting.

Let's go buy a painting. What can we afford that the kids won't
hate and throw out?

Welcome to My Haiku!

A haiku is a short poem,
often seventeen syllables
in three ordered lines
of five, seven, and five syllables.

Traditional haiku calls to mind a particular season.

The poem satisfies by bringing the reader
to a greater awareness of the natural world
and a deeper understanding
of the behavior, feelings, and experiences
of its human inhabitants.

Senryu is poetry which follows the haiku form
but calls up human nature rather than Mother Nature.

Senryu is often humorous.

A short poem includes a poetic turn
designed to surprise.

A haiku is spoken in the span of a single breath.

A poem avoids distractions
which take the reader out of the poem
and into observation of its construction.

If you find yourself counting on your fingers
to confirm the poem conforms
to the five-seven-five syllable structure,
you are missing the haiku.

I find it best to ignore rules of poetry.

What America Is

(after the poetry of an immigrant)

Finally freed from the terror of more
disappeared uncles, ghost children, and skeleton fathers,
the immigrant is living the dream
where cheeses are to be eaten
and not only to be found behind glass in museums.

She's on a mission to assure assimilation
of this new culture into her father's dreams.

I drink in her joy like lemon-lime soda,
her words sweet, tart, and bubbly.

I savor what she has discovered,
immersion in roses and artworks and music and Manhattan,
the open share of written expression.

She owns time for the first time.
America is not just free speech and opportunity.
America is a place where we can futz around if we feel like it.

What Fun

What fun is it, if all the words in a poem
are already hewn and hasped,
spackled and sanded,
neatly manicured and polished,
wrapped in gold foil,
tied with curled pink ribbon,
daubed with perfume,
and their cheeks pinched rosy?

I'd rather iron a poem as I read it,
pick the nits from the folds,
pop the last stubborn ice cube from the tray,

shake the branches,
release stubborn, colored dead leaves,

jigsaw that last piece into the puzzle,
scrape the gum from the bottom of its shoe,
and pull the extraneous from between the words
as a farmer's wife pulls scraggly weeds
from her vegetable garden,
stirs the soup, smells the stew,
and feeds her family the pumpkin pie.

I struggle with the rocks
which block the carrots from reaching all the way to China.

I bash rocks into sand, pulverize them into dust
and add glue and crayons.
I pour the whole mess out onto the grass behind the shed.

I wait to give it a name
until it is baked by the sun and the colors run together.

I wrassle with it — I *wrassle* with it ——we **wrassle!**
until it succumbs to my clever maneuvering
or it bests me and I cry, "Uncle!"

What Haven't I Done?

I read in a poem, "the tame woods of northwestern
New Jersey."

"Tame."

Wait, what?

I took my kids camping! in the wild! in real tents!
In the forest! And we hiked steep mountains!

In northwestern New Jersey.

We hid in the car from ravenous bears!
We ran from raccoons!
Squirrels!
Geese!
Deer ticks!
Poison ivy!
Mosquitos!
Black flies!
Swarms of vicious gnats!

We had to pee in outhouses!—with enormous, hairy, eight-eyed
spiders! And rough toilet paper!

And no night lights!

And our flashlight batteries ran out!

We were lucky to have survived
the "tame" woods
of northwestern New Jersey.

What Is This Terrifying Thing You Call "Hunger"?

Piercing screams label this interruption as urgent, more
important than the sleep required for mom's survival.
Hunger for milky is not at issue. Nursing went off
under normal constraints not too long ago. Reassurance
is required immediately, acknowledgment that panic is
real and the attacking rat or bat or bobcat would have
been dealt with immediately, had one existed, and any
and all would-be-harmers will be exterminated, should
any materialize. At the moment, there is no indication
that immediate action need be taken to remediate any
dangerous situation. All is safe, Baby Lee. Someday,
I will read to you the story of "Peter and the Wolf." You
will learn to read, too, every word. I will always be there
to explain the meaning of words you do not understand
and to hold you, rock you, kiss you, and sing to you.
I promise you my endless patience and fathomless love
as you find your way, your own way, from darkness
into the light.

While the Winds Howl

The winds howl tonight.

The coyote is silent,
belly full, sleeping soundly.

On waking, a great inhalation
brings fresh whiff of the scared.

A doe stands silently
beside her just-dropped fawn.

She hopes
for newborn legs to unfold,

to quickly learn to run.

White Hot Love

When the one you love is not strong,
and your love is streaming white-hot,
and you walk gingerly on eggshells,

and your promise to cherish for life
is not an emptied, corked wine bottle
floating in the waves,
waiting for a kid to read the note inside,

and your white diamonds are imaginary
and glisten more fiercely than the sun
or a million supernovas
or the Nagasaki gift of death,

and your furnace continues to burn
white hot throughout the night,
despite the death of the stoker,

the first fresh-white snow,
claiming to be the onset of winter,
holds no power to chill.
Crackling noises underfoot
are too soft to hear above
the white tempest, the roaring,
white-capped, whipping ocean,
and the resounding claps of repeating thunder
applauding the sky's streaking electric show.

This love storm, white with sheet lightning,
might torment and taunt,
but, it cannot wrench a shadow from the night
and spill it onto my heart.

My blazing, white-hot flaming heat burns inside,
lighting all the universe, just for you.

White Lies

One of humanity's original sins was to create stories.
The lie was born, spawn of love and pain.

A child we love cannot die, not now, not eventually.

We tell ourselves stories of Heaven,
of the loving God who would not let a child's death happen.

It is impossible that we could lose a child to death.
It cannot happen.
A child cannot die, but only goes to wait for us
to join them.

I know a lie when I hear one.

Yet, even so,
I must believe.
A child cannot die.
My own child cannot die,
not ever.

My heart rends reason,
and I believe.

I'm in awe of those
who first wrote lies
with such abandon,
who first used words
as tools of compassion.

Why I Don't Teach Poetry

Q.

What is a "poem"?

A.

A poem is what results
when a person informed by poetry concepts
commits word-wrangling.

Q.

What are "poetry concepts"?

A.

Poetry concepts are defined,
but not pinned down, nor cornered,
nor tortured into conformity.
Sorry, I can't be more specific.

Q.

What is "word-wrangling"?

A.

Move on, please. Nothing
to see here. Nothing
to see. Nothing.
No. Nope.
Nope.
No.

Why I Sleep More Easily Each Night

Every day, as my head hits the pillow,
crouched in guilt, remorse, and doubt
in the worthiness of my next breath,
I am more easily eased into sleep,

refreshed, even before sleep,
by my remembrance of the deepness of the doubt
that had enveloped me the night before

and, by morning,
had dissipated

into surety
there was so much more yet to be discovered

there were songs
yet to be sung

there were strings
I could not see or feel
but sensed existed

and stretched to the extremities
of either ends of time

and connected me to the beings
of what is
and of what doesn't exist, but only as possibility.

Why I've Had a Hard Time Getting Back to the YMCA Since My Mother Died

To me, "YMCA" means "Your Mother's Calling Again"

to insist

Don't waste that!
Don't you know leftovers are good food?
I don't care what you think it tastes like!
Do you think money grows on trees?

to question

Why haven't you started earning a salary again?
Don't you remember what I told you?
Relying on a man for financial support?
With four children at home!
Do you think that's what smart women do?
If you need an example, just look at your own mother!
If a man can do it all, why can't a woman?
She just makes up her mind, and she does it!

to demand

Listen! (As if I didn't hear her the first time.)
You still choose to disagree with me?
You open your clever mouth!
Why do I bother?
It's like arguing with a brick wall!

to swear

You should have been a lawyer because you can argue!
Like you're right and the whole world is wrong?
The whole world is not wrong!
Why can't you get that through your thick head?
Stop trying to twist every word to get what you want!

176

Words of Love

We never go anywhere, we're too cheap.

We believe in saving money.

It sounds nice,
but we can't afford it.

Sure, one of these days,
when we have money.

Good thing we never spend any money.

How much did you say that cost?

I can't believe people spend money
on that kind of thing.

Good thing we don't need anything.

My old one is good enough for now.

I don't need one,
but you go ahead if you'd like.

I don't need anything for my birthday.

Why would anyone buy one of those?

No, thanks, I'd hate to waste the money.

I'm happy, whatever we do together,
but let's try not to spend too much.

We don't spend money.

You Know That Feeling

You know that feeling when you're in the doctor's office with
your very dear loved ones and the doctor is already running
three hours late and you're all chatting wildly because you can
and you are laughing telling the story of that time when you all
went down the shore and how you were surprised by a wave
and wound up with seawater up your nose and a terrible
sunburn but survived and wasn't that the time our middle sister
couldn't make it because she had started medical school and we
all missed her but we were so proud and happy at her
graduation and because of that cruise coming up on Mother's
Day we all need to learn how to say "Where's the bathroom?"
and "More wine, please!" in French and then somebody makes
a joke out of a multi-lingual pun and we're all in hysterics and
then the doctor comes in and says the magic words

complete remission

and no one needs to change the expression on their face
because they're already so happy having so much fun with their
very dear loved ones and life is already so sweet and it couldn't
get any better than that? And then it does? Yeah, that feeling.
I already got what I want for Christmas.

Thank you for reading *My Husband's Roses*

AUTHOR

*It's amazing to think Susanna Lee hasn't changed a bit
since her college yearbook photo.*

—no one ever

Susanna Lee is a writer from the rural area in northern New Jersey where drivers stop to give bears crossing the road the right of way. Her work has been published in *brevitas, First Literary Review – East, Sensations Magazine, The Red Wheelbarrow, The Stillwater Review, The World According to Twitter, Voices From Here 2,* and her first book of poetry, *Sunrise Mountain,* 2015, which is now out of print. The volumes of Lee's collected works, published by Rose Mason Press as the *Cubist Poetry Series,* offer the reader a kaleidoscopic view of her writing. The first printing, in 2021, was a "Pandemic Panic!" version. The author was not sure she would not be touched by the contagion, but wanted her admittedly imperfect words to survive: she set them free in haste. She has since reworked the books, rewriting and vanquishing typos – at least, most of them – for this 2022 printing. *Snow Balls* consists of short stories, many autobiographical. *Great Blue Heron* is a collection of 5-7-5 haiku arranged in mini-chapbooks on themes such as pop culture, nursery rhymes, and art history—and with a bonus: haiku suitable for including in greeting cards on every special occasion. Lee's poems, sonnet length and shorter, appear in *Twisted Carrot;* poems longer than one page are in *God Laughs;* and her one-page poems are in *My Husband's Roses.* Lee's family recipes are preserved in *Fluffy Muffins,* which includes a section of instructions in kitchen basics for new cooks. Lee celebrates her love of music in bringing to print a newly discovered manuscript written eighty years ago by a friend's uncle, Jerome Bengis. Included with the found monograph, *Beethoven and His Nine Symphonies,* was a Forward by professor of music Edward Dickinson. Bengis' nephew Michael Bengis added a Preface; Lee added an Introduction and an Afterword and gave the book its title, *Genius in 9 Symphonies.*

In Gratitude

Thank you to my teachers, my family and friends, my poetry family, and especially Jim Klein, my poetry sensei, and Ashi Akira, my first haiku muse. My writing has flourished because of you all: your kindness, technical guidance, generous feedback, patience, and love.

A special thank you to members of my poetry workshops, including fellow poet Jennifer Poteet, who helped proofread the earliest drafts of this series.

I have enjoyed the open mic at events held at or sponsored by Betty June Silconas Poetry Center, Black Dog Books, brevitas, Broad Street Books, Carriage House Poetry Series, Center for Prevention and Counseling, Gainville Café, Great Weather for Media, Hudson Valley Writers Center, Luna Parc, North Jersey Literary Series, Pagoda Writers, Parkside Lounge, Paulinskill Poetry Project, Poetry at the Barn, Poetry Center at Passaic County Community College, Poets of the Palisades, Red Wheelbarrow Poets, *Sensations Magazine* Creative Events Series, Sussex County Community College, Tea and Conversation, Tea NJ, Thursdays Are for Poetry, White Space, Women Reading Aloud, Writers' Roundtable of Sussex County, NJ, and bookstores, colleges, clubs, and public libraries throughout the Tri-State region.

I'm deeply grateful to all who have invited me to be a featured reader or to speak on the subject of poetry, and to the Sparta Women's Club for asking me to read a poem to represent them at the NJ state competition for the performing arts.

I wish to thank editors who have chosen to include my work in their publications, and social media for allowing me to freely share my words, now and into the future, worldwide.

Thank you to my cousin CJ Rhoads, for her enthusiastic faith in my writing, and to her non-profit organization HPL Institute, Inc. for publishing my work and for doing good in the world.

Thank you to all who have ever read or heard me share my words and have offered feedback and/or encouragement.

All who have shared with me poetry and stories from their own lives have freed me to share mine. I hope my words now help free other voices. Write, and share.

PRIOR PUBLICATION

Brookes, Paul, ed. *The Wombwell Rainbow*, blog, 2020
    October 10. https://thewombwellrainbow.com
Crews, David, ed. *The Stillwater Review*, Volume 9. Betty June
    Silconas Poetry Center, 2019.
Fogarty, Mark, ed. *The Red Wheelbarrow 9*. White Chickens
    Press, 2016.
---. *The Red Wheelbarrow 10*. White Chickens Press, 2017.
---. *The Red Wheelbarrow 11*. White Chickens Press, 2018.
---. *The Red Wheelbarrow 12*. White Chickens Press, 2019.
---. *The Red Wheelbarrow 13*. White Chickens Press, 2020.
---. *The Red Wheelbarrow Poem of the Week*. White Chickens
    Press, 2017.
---. *The Red Wheelbarrow Poem of the Week 2*. White Chickens
    Press, 2018.
---. *The Red Wheelbarrow Poem of the Week 3*. White Chickens
    Press, 2019.
---. *The Red Wheelbarrow Poem of the Week 4*. White Chickens
    Press, 2020.
LeBlanc, Jean, ed. *Voices From Here 2*. The Paulinskill Poetry
    Project LLC, 2017.
MacLeod, Selene, and Jordan Gallader, eds. *Anthem: A Tribute
    to Leonard Cohen*. Nocturnicorn Books, 2017.
Messineo, David, ed. Dance, *Sensations Magazine*,
    Supplement 9. David Messineo, 2019.
---. Decade of Dichotomy, Feb. 1, 2011 – Jan. 31, 2021,
    Sensations Magazine, Supplement 11. David Messineo,
    2021.
---. Global Warming, *Sensations Magazine*, Supplement 10.
    David Messineo, 2020.
---. The Gathering Storm, *Sensations Magazine*, Supplement 6.
    David Messineo, 2017.
---. Westward Expansion, 1784-1959, *Sensations Magazine,*
    Supplement 8. David Messineo, 2019.
Pogue, David. *The World According to Twitter*. Black Dog &
    Leventhal, 2009.
Redus, Glenn, ed., *The Shinbone Star*, blog, 2020 March 23.
    https://exjournalistsunite.wordpress.com.

PRIOR PUBLICATION (CONT.)

Sostchen-Hochman, Cindy, and Karen Neuberg, eds. *First Literary Review – East*. September 2019. http://www.rulrul.4mg.com.

The 14th Annual brevitas Festival of the Short Poem. First Street Press, 2017.

The 15th Annual brevitas Festival of the Short Poem. First Street Press, 2018.

The 16th Annual brevitas Festival of the Short Poem. First Street Press, 2019.

The 17th Annual brevitas Festival of the Short Poem. First Street Press, 2020.

Winners of The White Shoe Haiku Contest, *The White Shoe Irregular*, 2000 November 27. http://www.whiteshoe.org/archive/001127haiku1.html.

Winners of The White Shoe Haiku Contest, *The White Shoe Irregular*, 2001 January 16. http://www.whiteshoe.org/archive/001127haiku1.html.

Published by Rose Mason Press

Cubist Poetry Series: 6 volumes

by Susanna Lee

Great Blue Heron: Haiku
Twisted Carrot: Petite Poems
My Husband's Roses: One-Page Poems
God Laughs: Longer Poems
Snow Balls: Short Stories
Fluffy Muffins: Recipes for My Peeps

Genius in 9 Symphonies: How Beethoven Reinvented Music

by Jerome Bengis

Sunrise Mountain: Haiku and Other Poetry

by Susanna Lee

Made in the USA
Middletown, DE
20 September 2022

73499822R00109